24 Keys
That Bring
Complete
Success

Complete
Success

"One of America's greatest entrepreneurs reflects on what you will carry across the finish line. Paul Meyer has written the Cliff Notes for how a successful businessman can lead a Christ-directed life. Highly recommended."

Patrick Morley, men's author and President of Man in the Mirror

"Paul J. Meyer practices what he preaches. His life has influenced and touched my life for more than two decades!"

Michael Youssef, Ph.D., Host of the Radio and TV program Leading the Way with Dr. Michael Youssef

"Paul J. Meyer is the 21st century 'guru' for personal development for mind and spirit. His books and materials for self-help efforts have recently reached its highest pinnacle for helping people reach their highest potential."

Gil A. Stricklin, Founder & President of Marketplace Ministries, Inc. Dallas, Texas

"One of the greatest blessings in my 50+ years in Christ has been witnessing God's power, love, and wisdom manifested through his servant, Paul J. Meyer. His stewardship and achievements are an inspiration to millions, and especially me."

Charlie T. Jones, Author of Life is Tremendous

"As a business associate and personal friend, I have known Paul for more than 30 years. He is a man of influence and inspiration. His programs have not only helped me but also thousands of others in Japan to develop personally in every area of their lives. I personally appreciate his influence on my decision to become a Christian in 1987 and since then the rest of my family: my wife, my children, and my grandchildren."

Hei Arita, President, PJM Japan Co., Ltd.

24 Keys
That Bring
Complete
Success

Complete
Success

Paul J. Meyer

Bridge-Logos

Gainesville, FL 32614 USA

Bridge-Logos

Gainesville, FL 32614 USA

24 Keys That Bring Complete Success
by Paul J. Meyer

Printed in the United States of America.

Library of Congress Catalog Card Number: 2005936839
International Standard Book Number 0-88270-108-8

Unless othewise noted, all Scripture quotations are taken from the Holy Bible: New King James Version © 1979, 1980, 1982, Thomas Nelson, Inc., Publishers.

G163.316.N.m601.352100

Dedication

To my wife Jane: you are the most balanced person on earth and the joy of my life! You have helped me find real success.

To my children Jim, Larry, Billy, Janna, and Leslie: you make this dad proud!

To my grandchildren Mike, Brady, Cole, Allison, Jason, Jessica, Jennifer, Joshua, Adam, Christie, Morgan, Brooke, Kelsey, Jordan, and Jaden: I look forward to your future!

To my parents, August Carl Meyer (1892-1963) and Isabelle Rutherford Meyer (1892-1969): your success lives on!

To my sister Elizabeth (1926-1999) and brother Carl: hardly a day goes by that I don't reflect on the times we enjoyed together.

And to everyone I have ever met or will meet through these pages: your success is of your making, unlimited, and able to change the world!

Contents

Foreword
by John C. Maxwell

Let me take this opportunity to express my highest regard for Paul J. Meyer and for what he stands for. He has made an enormous impact in my life and I will always be grateful for that.

I first heard of Paul in 1970. I was a young man, just out of seminary and recently married, still finding my feet as a new pastor. I was invited to a presentation on how to set and achieve goals, hosted by a company I had never heard of before, Success Motivation Institute, Inc.

Looking back, it was as if that night I traded in my chuck wagon for a bullet train. My eyes were opened to the reality of living in the world of the "impossible," setting goals, and taking giant steps toward my destiny. I was so impressed that I knew I needed to immerse myself in the principles outlined in Paul's course, but the cost was more than I could afford at the time. I immediately went home and asked my wife Margaret what we could cut out of our budget so I could buy the course.

We bought the course and it profoundly affected my ministry and my career for Christ. I often think of that crucial night and am grateful for the effort that Paul went through to write out those principles and to make it available for everyone.

A few years ago I had the opportunity to have dinner with Paul and his wife Jane at a restaurant in southern California. One of the first things I said was, "You never let your hero pay for dinner." He asked what I meant and I explained the impact he had made on my life. He was touched, and so was I.

For decades I have used his materials, either for myself or for leaders across the nations, and am always amazed at the changes that take place in people's lives. But I should know better—everything Paul puts his hands to is life-changing!

I see this book as the condensed version of everything that Paul has believed, practiced, and taught for more than 50 years. In addition, he is one of those rare individuals who actually does what he says he will do! In fact, he keeps track of his promises and puts them in a vault and then at the end of the year incorporates them into his will! His word is as good as gold—even better!

He has taken seriously the fact that *"a good man leaves an inheritance to his children's children"* (Proverbs 13:22) and understands that this means much more than just a financial inheritance. He is the first to point out that every area of life is vitally important for real success.

As you read Paul's wisdom, advice, and personal stories, keep in mind that he has already done what he is talking about. He isn't talking theory—he's talking reality!

Regardless of any limitation we might place on ourselves, we have an incredible opportunity to learn from someone who has charted a course before us. Take it and run!

Paul, it is a joy and an honor to write these words of appreciation and recommendation. You are more than qualified to write this book and I have no doubt that that book will motivate thousands of readers to reach a level of success that others could only dream about.

Thank you again for playing a part in my life those many years ago.

Admiringly,

John C. Maxwell

Introduction

WHAT IS SUCCESS?

Is it money?
Is it freedom?
Is it power?
Is it influence?

The answer is "yes" to all of the above, but don't stop there! Real success is so much more!

What is real success? How do you find it? How do you get it? All good questions, but you'll have to read the entire book to find the answers.

I have been a student of success for decades and found that success begins with a choice. It is up to you. You have the right and the ability to be successful, but success comes after you first choose to succeed.

Think of it like this: you have a key in your hand that opens a door to untold success. You choose whether or not you will open that door. It's your choice. It's up to you.

That is why the chapters in this book are called Success Keys. I used these keys to achieve more than I ever dreamed, imagined, or even wanted. I've found what is truly most important in life and am daily in awe of the unlimited success that still lied ahead!

The incalculable potential for success is the very reason that I wrote this book. I wanted you, the reader, to tap into the same potential that I tapped into, only to an even larger degree! You can if you choose to.

I also wrote this book for my children and grandchildren as well as for every associate, employee, friend, acquaintance, and for the people who have bought our programs for the last 40+ years.

It is my hope, desire, and prayer that you will be encouraged and equipped to excel beyond your highest expectations in every area of life!

May these success keys open the doors before you!

It's Your Attitude!

Discovering the keys for ALL success

Early on in my insurance career I recruited some incredibly gifted and talented people, only to find that they had developed or been programmed with negative mental attitude and could not produce.

Repetitively dealing with people who needed a complete attitude overhaul showed me the importance of attitude and was the underlying inspiration behind my first company, Success Motivation International. I've been called the "founder of the personal development industry"—*and it all started with attitude!*

Attitude is a habit of thought, so if you want to change your attitude, you must change the way you think.

Attitude is who you are

Who you are is *not* determined by how you look, where you live, or who your parents were. *Who you are is a function of specific choices that you have made.* You are where you are and what you are because of the dominating thoughts in your mind. After all, as a man *"thinks in his heart, so is he"* (Proverbs 23:7).

A plastic surgeon friend of mine made a study of the people on whom he had performed cosmetic surgery. He gave them new noses, took away their wrinkles, or made some other significant changes in their appearances. But he discovered something quite unexpected.

Most of the people thought the surgery had been a failure because they were still dissatisfied with themselves.

The conclusion is obvious. *We are what we think we are—not what we appear to be on the outside.*

The effect of your attitude on you

As a young man, I knew in my heart that I would not do manual labor (i.e., picking fruit) for the rest of my life. On the inside I was different than those around me, and over time, the outside lined up with what my inside believed. Changes on the outside will inevitably match what the heart and mind have already decided to do or be.

Each of us has an overall pattern of thinking that is generally either positive or negative. The pattern you choose has four profound effects on your life:

> "We can alter our lives by altering our attitudes of mind."
> William James

#1) Your basic attitude affects your belief in your potential for success. A negative attitude causes you to doubt your ability to achieve, while belief in your potential makes you willing to take the necessary action for success.

#2) Your attitude determines how you perceive a challenge. A positive attitude lets you see a challenge as an opportunity rather than a threat.

#3) Your attitude determines your confidence. People with negative attitudes think, "I can't ..." or "I doubt ..." In contrast, each time you act from a positive attitude, your self-confidence is enhanced, your ability to achieve is proven, and you know you can succeed.

#4) Your attitude affects how you see opportunity. People who have negative attitudes have buried the ability to see opportunity. A positive attitude opens your eyes to so many opportunities that your challenge becomes which opportunity to choose.

How to form attitudes
To form an attitude, the first step is input. Everything since birth is used by your subconscious mind as input from which attitudes are formed. You obviously can't start over at birth. What you can do, however, is change the input. This has a way of positively affecting your mind and your entire body, as Scripture clearly states, *"Be transformed by the renewing of your mind"* (Romans 12:2).

The second step in the formation of attitudes is **personal processing of inputs**. You heard what others said, watched what they did, and processed that information and chose your attitudes. As you acted on your chosen belief, it gradually became a habit of thought—an attitude.

> To change your attitude, you must change the way you think.

My chosen belief is that I can do anything. **I wake up each day without the mental recognition of the possibility of defeat.** It affects everything I do, say, or think.

The final element is **reinforcement**. When you choose an attitude, it becomes firmly entrenched as you follow it day after day.

These three steps work beautifully together, but suppose that some specific attitude is holding you back from the success you are capable of attaining. Can you change that attitude? **Yes, you can!**

Changing an attitude is not simple or necessarily quick, but it is certainly possible. *You must first make a conscious choice to change!* The following principle hits the nail right on the head:
- Sow a thought, reap an action,
- Sow an action, reap a habit,
- Sow a habit, reap character,
- Sow character, reap a destiny.

Three big changes: Thought, Speech, and Behavior
Attitudes operate on three planes: thoughts, speech, and behavior. What you fill your mind with is eventually translated into the words

you speak, and then your words create action. You can intervene in the process of attitude formation at any one of the three points: thoughts, speech, or behavior.

#1 Work on your thoughts.

Whenever you catch yourself thinking, "I can't" or "I'm afraid," stop and tell yourself, "Look again. I'll give this opportunity a chance. I can do it!"

Or make up your own success message, such as, "I know I can do this" or "I am, without question, the right person to do this!"

The important thing to do is to *break the automatic negative thought pattern.*

> "Immense power is acquired by assuring yourself in your secret reveries that you were born to control affairs."
> Andrew Carnegie

#2 Change your speech patterns.

How often do you use negative words or express doubt, lack of confidence in your ability, or fear?

Write out some positive words to use the next time the chance arises. Be sure these words express the kind of success attitude you want to adopt. Practice long enough that you will remember the positive words when you need them.

#3 Modify behavior.

A friend of mine was given a challenging project at work. Instead of getting started, he went and slouched in front of the TV. When he realized what he was doing, he made the conscious effort to get up and begin the project. Intervening at the point of behavior is often the easiest point at which you can begin to make a change.

Where you intervene is up to you, since your personality is unique and your abilities are different.

How to intervene

One of the most effective ways to intervene is to make use of the Power Mind Principle to change your attitude, which involves using a highly controlled practice of visualization, according to a specific plan, designed to accomplish a definite purpose.

Here is how it works:

A) Begin by spending some time in quiet relaxation. Put side worries, fears, and anxieties for the moment.

B) Read some written text that describes the attitude or belief you *want to adopt.*

C) Actively visualize yourself acting, speaking, or feeling in accordance with that attitude or belief.

D) Finally, through visualization, actually experience the behavior.

Attitudes, because they are habits of thought, do not happen overnight. *Give yourself time to absorb enough new, positive input to make the desired change.* Plan positive reinforcement to reward yourself when you succeed. Positive affirmations serve this purpose well, a few of which are:

- I see progress already.
- I am willing to persist to see greater change!
- My plan is working—I will succeed!

Measure your progress by comparing where you are now to where you were when you started. This encourages you to continue your efforts to grow by proving that growth is possible. Being thankful for your progress is an important part of the reinforcement process.

Benefits of a positive attitude
The benefits of a positive attitude are outstanding:
1. increased enthusiasm
2. freedom from the limitations of fear
3. increased creativity
4. enjoyment in taking the initiative
5. joy when using more of your God-given potential
6. boundless opportunities
7. abundance of positive friends and colleagues

8. increased efficiency in utilizing your time and energy

Will you still make mistakes? Yes, of course, but there is more profit in making a few mistakes than in avoiding them altogether. Those who have too great a fear of making mistakes will take no risks and so will not grow or learn.

Depending on your attitude, every obstacle, and challenge has the potential to be the best thing that ever happened to you.

It's your attitude!

> "We are what we repeatedly do; excellence, then, is not an act, but a habit."
>
> Aristotle

Living Life with an Attitude of Gratitude

Because life is what you make of it

From birth to the grave we are insulted, left out, taken advantage of, and discounted by others, let alone the negative things that naturally happen in life! But when you view your world with an attitude of gratitude, you are training yourself to focus on the good in life.

Of the 100 companies I've started since the age of 19, 65 percent have not survived. They could be called "failures," but with my positive attitude, I've never considered that I've failed at anything.

These "failures" were only temporary setbacks and I learned to be grateful for each one. *I know that in every adversity there is a seed of equivalent or greater benefit if I believe it, look for it, and work for it.*

These "failures" enabled me to study why the concept, business, or idea did not work. What's more, I was mentally tougher and smarter going into the next situation. How could I not be grateful?

When you place the bad beside the good, the negative beside the positive, you gain a whole new perspective about life.

> "Learning to be thankful covers it all."
>
> Charlie "Tremendous" Jones

Here are just a few examples:

• My dad wouldn't let me buy a model airplane at the hobby shop. He showed me how to design and build my own from raw materials and I won awards for it!

• My dad wouldn't let me buy my first bicycle. I learned how to restore old bicycles and made money doing it!

• My first job in the insurance industry was starting at the very bottom. I had the privilege of starting as an apprentice and learning it from the bottom!

• I had a lot of competition from others at work. I worked harder and performed better because of the competition!

The bad/negative times were a perfect breeding ground for success and breakthrough. Instead of letting the hard times get me down, I've learned to keep going and to look for the hidden good.

Count your blessings

The classic hymn that says, "Count your blessings, name them one by one …" couldn't be more valid.

I know a family that writes down all the things they are grateful for in a special notebook on a monthly basis. As they review each month's entries, they are training themselves and their children to view life through eyes of gratefulness.

> "Life is rich in rewards to a person who has learned to be thankful in any and every circumstance."
>
> Bill Bunting

Writing something down dramatically increases your chances of remembering it. But whether you write it down, memorize it, re-read it, or make it into a song, do whatever you have to do to be grateful! The Bible records multiple instances where the Israelites *"forgot His works"* (i.e., Psalms 78:11) and reverted back to their former attitudes and actions. They forgot!

It is our nature to forget. That is, however, no excuse for forgetting.

Being grateful requires positive recall

One of the few times it is healthy to look back is when you are being grateful. Usually, looking back will slow you down or trip you up. Here are six of the many things that I'm grateful for:

#1 Family

My parents: Together they taught me to live, to dream, and to be disciplined enough to get where I wanted to go. They showed me by example that if I could control my heart and mind, I could control my actions and therefore my future. By denying me the easy way out, they were forcing me to learn how to free myself.

> "Ingratitude is the essence of vileness."
> Immanuel Kant
> (1724-1804)

My wife: Jane is my best friend. She knows me, the inner me, and she loves me all the more. I often say that when I grow up I want to be like her, and I mean it!

My children: My five children make me the proudest father in the world and my grandchildren are icing on the cake! They have all made the most important decision possible, accepting Jesus into their hearts, and they are all growing and maturing in their areas of influence.

#2 Friends

I have had countless friends over the years who have been there when I needed them most. One friend gave me a handful of cash when I needed it desperately, another listened to me vent my frustrations about life and told me he believed in me and that I ought to pursue my dreams, and others have been honest enough to tell me when I needed to change.

#3 Protection and favor

I've walked away from many potentially deadly accidents, including three plane crashes. That makes me believe God has a special purpose for my life.

He also grants me favor with people. I've gone into businesses and been greeted with, "I don't know what you are selling, but I'm going to buy some." Other times I've been in the right place at the right time and overheard a business deal that turned out to be highly lucrative for me. I could have been 10 seconds late or early and missed it all!

#4 Hard times

Hard times can bring good character. Extreme pressure as a salesman caused me to fly higher, fight stronger, and stay longer than the competition. Pressure on carbon produces a diamond over time, and I've come to accept pressure as a good thing *because I know the value of all that is being refined in me.*

> In every adversity there is a seed of equivalent or greater benefit if you believe it, look for it, and work for it.

A Russian proverb states, "The same hammer that shatters the glass forges the steel." If we have positive attitudes, adversities and difficulties can only make us a stronger and more confident. Hard times may bring good character, but "hard times" are not synonymous with "bad days."

#5 Answered prayers

Countless times I have prayed for the impossible concerning people, relationships, jobs, etc., and found that God has done more than I could have asked or imagined. It is interesting to note that we are commanded in Scripture to *"continue earnestly in prayer, being vigilant in it with thanksgiving"* (Colossians 4:2). Thanksgiving and prayer go hand in hand.

#6 Forgiveness, love and mercy

Most importantly, I am grateful for what God has done for me. Words cannot express my appreciation for Him sending His Son to die on the cross for me. And not only did He make a way for me to receive forgiveness of my sins and be restored to Him, He planted people in my life who told me about Christ.

What Jesus did for me is incredible, but the fact that He told me about it through other people shows me just how much He cares for me. Advances in technology are enabling us to discover galaxies where we first thought only a few stars were located. In the vastness of it all, the Creator has singled me out! *That is truly amazing!*

Living with an attitude of gratitude is without a doubt the best way to live life.

Your Positive Self-image

How you see yourself is how others see you

One absolutely essential ingredient for success is that of a positive self-image. The world operates on the basis of the law of attraction: *what you are and what you think will attract corresponding conditions.*

If you have a negative self-image, you attract negative results. If your self-image is positive, you attract positive results. This may appear simplistic, *but it is absolutely true!*

What is your self-image?
Your self-image is your mental picture of yourself comprised of six important ingredients:

1. what you believe about your talents and abilities
2. what you believe about your worth as a person
3. how you expect others to accept you
4. what you believe you can become
5. what you expect your world to be like
6. what you believe about how you came into existence

Your mental picture of yourself determines the measure of confidence you bring to using your potential and working toward your goals.

> The image you portray is the image you have of yourself.

Psychologists estimate we use **less than** a third of our actual potential. By increasing your potential just slightly, you can make a sizable improvement in your effectiveness. If you are now using 30 percent of your potential, you could choose to use an additional 3 percent, a total of 33 percent. This additional 3 percent is equal to 10 percent of what you were previously using. With relatively little effort, you can be 10 percent more effective than you are now.

Most of us have three separate self-images, which include:

A. **the "me" I really am** (your true potential)

B. **the "me" I think I am** (this depends upon how well you know yourself)

C. **the "me" I want to become** (can expand as you learn your true potential)

For me, I want to be the perfect husband (C: *who I want to become*) and sometimes I think I do a pretty good job (B: *who I think I am*), but to get the most accurate reading (A: *who I really am*), you would have to ask my wife.

> What you do is merely a result of who you are.

The closer these three images are, the better. People who have a distorted picture of their real inner being never discover their true potential.

Self-image is built day by day from experiences, from what other people say and do, and from how you respond to all of these occurrences. If you respond with the same emotion, feeling, or action every time you meet similar circumstances, that response becomes a habit and your subconscious mind files this as the kind of person you are.

Though some say we have no real control over our choices or that our choices are simply the result of past conditioning, *we do indeed have control over our choices!* Knowing that I can control my future motivates me, excites me, and gives me hope for a better tomorrow.

The truth is, we can build a new self-image (one that is a more accurate picture of our real, God-given potential) the same way we built our present self-image—*by exercising our power of choice.*

Can I really change my self-image?

Your mind works like a computer, storing the information you give it and using this information to formulate your thoughts, which means A) your present (who you are and where you are today) is a result of your past choices and B) your future will be the result of what you are thinking about and choosing now

Your self-image is the result of all you have given your subconscious mind as a database, so, regardless of your background, what you are willing to become is the only reality that counts. And that depends greatly upon what you believe and what you are willing to do about your self-image.

Some people allow artificial barriers to limit their potential success. I believe it is because they have let one or more of the following 7 attitudes hinder their potential:

1. **"I'm comfortable."** Remaining at present levels of success is easier and less stressful than making needed changes.

2. **"I'm afraid of failure."** Risking possible failure prohibits trying anything new.

3. **"Disapproval hurts."** Avoiding disapproval limits behaviors to those calculated to please.

4. **"I don't want to rock the boat."** Change is viewed as negative and too risky.

5. **"I don't have what it takes."** Belief that one does not deserve the rewards of using their full potential which is caused by a false sense of inferiority.

6. **"Success might not be good for me."** Unworthiness and an illogical fear of success causes the person to subconsciously avoid success.

7. **"God doesn't want me to succeed."** This unfounded belief sends many great dreams into tailspins. Scripture says, *"I pray that you may prosper in all things"* (3 John 2).

The success you seek can become reality when you exchange limiting beliefs for a more positive self-image.

How to strengthen your positive self-image

Choosing to strengthen your self-image is an amazing possibility and the benefits will last a lifetime. The following four-step plan will help strengthen your positive self-image:

1. Learn the power of dreams. Imagine something new or you will only go where you have been. Discover a dream that is so important you are willing to commit your life to it. Dreams give you the ability to see the possible, visualize it as the probable, and transform it into reality.

2. Cultivate a burning desire to reach your dreams. Desire kindles motivation, builds enthusiasm, sparks creativity, and triggers action. Cultivate desire by keeping your purpose and goals before you daily.

3. Exercise your freedom of choice. Act on your freedom to choose. If you hesitate, others will choose for you, directing you toward *their* goals, not yours. If you are fearful, choose courage. If you frequently procrastinate, choose to take action now. If you have always waited for others to lead, use your own initiative.

4. Learn who you are and what your Creator says you can do. Scripture says, *"If anyone is in Christ, he is a new creation"* (2 Corinthians 5:17) and, *"I can do all things through Christ who strengthens me"* (Philippians 4:13).

You've got what it takes

You already have all the raw material you need for your greatest dream of success. Consider a common chicken egg. That formless, gelatinous mass includes everything necessary for making a baby chick and feeding it until it is large enough to hatch even though you can see no traces of a beak, legs, bones, eyes, or feathers. When the time is right, the chick pecks a hole in the shell and begins to hatch. If someone tries to help, the chick seldom survives.

Even more astonishing is the potential within you to build any kind of future that you desire. Sadly, people often look to others to help them, protect them, and guide them. They are short-changing their personal potential. Only God has the wisdom and power to help each of us become all that we are intended to be.

Self-motivation is the sharp beak you use to break out of the shell that limits your full potential. I have seen some people focus on maximizing their potential while others of equal talent and ability choose not to.

> No self-image will ever be maximized without Jesus Christ. It is simply impossible.

By taking charge of your life, you are exercising the initiative to discover the great pool of talents and abilities that make up your inner being. As you remove the padlocks from those qualities that have been locked away from your awareness, your full potential will become available.

You have at your disposal the same resources given to any great achiever. Life is an orchestra and you have the baton to direct the interpretation of life's song. You have the same 8 notes of the scale given to Mozart, Bach, and Chopin.

Life is a painting and you are the artist. You have on your palette all the colors in the spectrum — the same ones available to Michaelangelo and DaVinci.

Life is an adventure story and you are the writer. You have the same 26 letters in the alphabet — the same ones used by Shelley, Milton, and Shakespeare.

You have it all! Use it to its full potential.

The Motivation of Goal Setting

Turning your dreams into reality

Goal setting is the most important aspect of all improvement and personal development plans. It is the key to all fulfillment and achievement. Confidence, determination, and innate personality traits contribute to success, but they all come into focus through goal setting.

Probably 75 percent of my personal success has come through setting goals (the other 25 percent is a combination of focus, desire, preparation, and hard work). If I'm not making the progress I would like to make and am capable of making, it is simply because my goals are not clearly defined.

There is something almost mystical about a crystallized goal after you have developed a plan and set a deadline for its attainment. Such a goal produces a burning desire, intense self-confidence, and a firm determination to follow through. Having a wild imagination is one thing, but being very disciplined and organized makes you different from the rest. *Many dream, but few dream and then fulfill.*

Anything is possible

Goal setting is simply writing down your dreams, crystallizing your thinking, and then developing a plan with a deadline for its attainment. Along the way, you *will* face obstacles, but overcoming adversities and temporary defeats will make you stronger. When you reach your goal you will have accomplished much more than you set out to do.

When I first started in the insurance business, my goal was to write a million dollars worth of business, *but I only made one sale out of 14 initial presentations!* My highest monthly income during the first nine months was $87. But I believed in my goal. Eventually I hit the million-dollar mark and the next year after that sold almost four million!

If you are self-motivated and goal-oriented, obstacles merely intensify your desire. Be thankful for obstacles because they push you closer to your goals.

The secret of people who accomplish their dreams

A survey taken a few years ago revealed that only 3 percent of people have written down their goals and are working toward them. Another 10 percent, equally as well educated and determined, do a great deal of thinking about their goals but they have not written them down. The first group outperformed the second group anywhere from 10-to-1 to 100-to-1.

A third group surveyed included more than 60 percent of the people. These average people set goals for extremely short-range objectives: the next raise, the next vacation, etc. They are just getting by financially and seldom take time to think outside their daily routine.

The balance of those surveyed (nearly 30 percent) had never considered what they wanted out of life. They are dependent or partially dependent on others for subsistence.

The top 3 percent wrote down their goals and that is what differentiates them from all the rest. Some call it a minor detail, but the difference between those at the top and the rest of society is anything but minor!

Unwritten goals are hazy goals and produce at best, hazy results. A written goal keeps you on track, serves as a checkpoint, and protects you from being overwhelmed by outside distractions.

The tendency of NOT setting goals

Those who fail to set goals are the very ones who need goals the most. They have great potential and could go to amazing heights, but they will never fulfill their potential.

Most people have difficulty setting goals. Whatever the reason or excuse, it is sad to see people far short of their potential. I have found that Christians are particularly bad at goal setting, despite the many examples of preparing, planning ahead, and leading that are found in the Bible. Noah spent years building the first boat *before* mankind had even witnessed rain. There are numerous other examples, all showing that God is into long-term growth, taking dominion, and hard work—and so should we be.

> "Those who are successful in any field are the goal setters. They have a desire to achieve that is coupled with discipline."
> Larry Burkett

Instead, we often give up control by allowing bad habits to form. For example, I constantly hear people saying, "I don't want to take over from God. I gave God my life, so He is the one in control" or "Jesus is coming soon, so I don't bother making any long-term plans."

To the first excuse: Until you are dead, you are responsible for your own life, and since it is your responsibility, you need to work hard and be faithful with what God has given you.

To the second excuse: Nobody knows the day or the hour of Christ's return (Matthew 25:13). We need to live like He isn't coming back in our lifetime. Then if He does, excellent! And if He doesn't, excellent! *When we live only for His return, we miss out on what He has in store for us now.*

Setting goals for your success

There are four different goals that play a part in your overall success. The first goal is the most common: the *short-range goal*. These goals range from today to six months from now. Focusing on the daily actions necessary to accomplish your goals will help you internalize the process.

The second goal is the *long-range goal*. Such goals range from one year to a lifetime and express your purpose for living.

The third goal is the *tangible goal*. These are needs and wants, such as increased income, a certain trip with the family, etc. You can see and feel them, which is often helpful in attaining these goals.

Married? You and your spouse must establish goals together.

The fourth goal is the most important: the *intangible goal*. These are goals that affect your personal character and can be spiritual, mental, emotional, etc. Usually the attainment of intangible goals (i.e., change in a certain character trait) precedes the reaching of a tangible goal. For example, when character and integrity are not properly developed, the tangible goals of owning a business or managing a larger income are usually short lived.

Write your goals down, no matter how silly they sound. Don't allow the motivational blocks in your past to limit your dreams or listen to voices that say, "I can't do that." *You can do absolutely anything you want!*

After your dreams are recorded, it's time to develop a plan for achieving them. **Use the 5-point Paul J. Meyer Personal Success Plan**, the criteria that I use to measure every goal I undertake. Ask:

1. Have I crystallized my thinking about this goal?
2. Do I have a plan and a deadline for its attainment?
3. Do I have a burning desire?
4. Do I have confidence in my ability to succeed?
5. Do I have an iron-willed determination to pay whatever price necessary to get the job done, regardless of circumstance, criticism, or what other people may say, think, or do?

When you answer "yes" to these five questions, then ask one more: "Is it worth it to me?"

If you are willing to invest the time, money, and effort required, then go after it! You have what it takes to accomplish your goal, no matter what happens, no matter who criticizes, no matter whether you have the money or not, and no matter what you now lack in experience.

"There is no security on this earth. There is only opportunity."
Douglas MacArthur

What motivates you?

The *results* and *benefits* of your goals motivate you. People without goals are not motivated to change. They only do what is comfortable and familiar simply because they've never done it another way and don't want to change now.

To reach *your* goals you must be willing to change. There are five factors to consider about your goals:

1. They must be *your* personal goals.
2. They must be *stated positively* instead of negatively.
3. They must be *written and specific*. Dreams are general, but plans get more and more specific.
4. They must be *realistic, compatible, and attainable*. Day-to-day planning needs to be realistic and fit within your value system.
5. They must include *basic personality changes*. "Being" comes before "having," which means the right habits and attitudes are required BEFORE goals can be achieved.

If you have been constricted and made to fit within pre-determined boundaries, then you must prepare to break out. It doesn't matter whoever or whatever is at fault. What matters is that you are liberated. Don't look back but keep your gaze straight ahead.

Whatever your goal, stick with it. Take responsibility, leave no room for the possibility of defeat, see obstacles as steps in the right direction, and keep feeding your mind with positives.

If I had allowed my mind to dwell on the negatives about my dismal sales performance in the insurance industry, I would have quit soon after I started. Instead, I believed I could do it, set concrete goals, and before long the expected thing happened: my sales began to increase!

Goal setting takes your dreams and turns them into reality.

Choices and Consequences

Saying "yes" also means saying "no"

What you choose will become your life, affecting you and everyone around you. That is because you possess one of the most powerful forces in the world: the power of choice.

There are four basic choices around which the rest of your world will rotate: 1) where you spend eternity, 2) whether you discover and pursue your God-given destiny, 3) who you marry, and 4) how you raise your children.

The first choice is about whether or not you have accepted Jesus as your Lord and Savior. His death on the cross gives everyone equal access to God's forgiveness and to heaven. Where you will spend eternity is always your choice.

The second choice relates to the first. God says, *"I know the thoughts that I think toward you ... thoughts of peace and not of evil, to give you a future and a hope"* (Jeremiah 29:11). However, you still have to make the choice to take Him at His word. Discovering His purpose for your life and living it out is the most exciting adventure possible!

The third choice can affect every area of life. The choice of a mate is not a decision to be made rashly! Let God bring the perfect mate to you at the right time.

The final choice is about how to raise your children. This is also vitally important because your children will continue your success.

In each of these choices, we all possess the same power to choose. How wisely you use that power is up to you.

Choices have consequences

Choices have consequences, whether good or bad. This may seem obvious, but people fail to grasp this reality.

The insurance company that fired me when I was young did themselves a great disservice. They said I was introverted when actually I was purposefully quiet because I was listening and learning from their best salesmen. They let me go after only three weeks. Within a few years I was selling circles around their best salesman, but their "yes" to firing me meant "no" to me ever working there again.

Consequences are not always bad. Winning an academic scholarship, reaching a sales goal, and making a wise investment could be termed "rewards," "profits," or even "luck," but you know otherwise. They are consequences from making right choices.

> The power of choices and consequences are not bound by money ... or the lack of it.

The natural principle of sowing and reaping is always at work. Whatever you plant, whether physical, spiritual, mental, financial, relational, or emotional, will grow and some day return to you in a multiplied fashion. It can be incredibly good or terribly bad, depending on your seed.

Learn one thing, gain another

When I was a boy, I desperately wanted a bicycle. Instead of buying me one, my dad took me to the junkyard where we selected several old bicycles. We took the "junk" to our garage where my dad showed me how to strip the bike down to its basic frame. Then he said, "Put it back together and you'll have a bicycle."

Sure enough, when all the parts were reassembled (he made me do it twice), I had a whole bicycle! I even learned how to strip the metal and repaint it. With this new knowledge, I suddenly found myself with a business opportunity. As a teenager I refurbished and sold over 300 bicycles!

By saying "no" to buying a new bicycle, I was saying "yes" to confidence, maturity, creativity, financial gain, and a whole lot more. By saying "yes" to the learning process, I was saying "no" to a I-deserve-it-so-give-it-to-me mentality. My father showed me that the power of choices and consequences were not bound by the money we did or did not have. That power was mine, and he showed me how to harness it. He helped me unlock the potential that I did not see in myself.

I tried to do the same with my children, though in a different manner. I took my five children fishing, hunting, golfing, SCUBA diving, water skiing, go-cart riding, and more. My son Billy, for example, must have had the best go-cart workshop in the country. He won numerous local competitions as a youngster and later went into professional auto racing.

According to my priorities, family always came first, and the consequences of that choice have been wonderful!

Minor choices, major impact

You never know how large the impact may be from a seemingly minor choice. For example, while on a family vacation cruise, the ship stopped briefly in the Cayman Islands. The captain said it was the prettiest of the eight stops the ship would make, so I replied, "OK, we'll get off here."

We spent the rest of our vacation right there! Since then, the Caymans have become the home office to several of our overseas businesses and proved to be one of the best choices we ever made, not to mention the location for many, unforgettable times as a family. One choice with many positive consequences!

When I was young and selling insurance, I sold a policy to a pilot who was about to move to California. He needed to sell his house and car quickly, so I bought his Cadillac by getting it financed at a local bank and bought his house by convincing the realtor to loan me the money. My new neighbor happened to be a young pastor by the name of Bill Hinson who later became one of my best friends and one of the biggest influences in my life.

Upon learning of my dissatisfaction with the insurance business, Bill told me about a record company in Waco, Texas that needed help with marketing and distribution. I ended up moving to Waco and helped turn the company around and have lived there ever since!

In short, I can't imagine how different my world would be if I had not made that one choice!

Today's choices bring tomorrow's results

An elderly Chinese entrepreneur from Hong Kong, Henry Tseung, flew to Waco to thank me for the impact I had made in his business. He greeted me in broken English, "You help me, now I help you. You do day's work; I observe."

> You never know how large the impact may be from a seemingly minor change.

All day Henry followed me everywhere I went. He listened to my phone calls, observed how I treated personnel, and sat in on my meetings. At one point Charles, our sales manager, came in to discuss a product. I told Charles what I wanted him to do, say, write, etc. When he left, Henry said, "Henry feel sorry for Charles because he become lesser person every time he see you."

Neither of us knew the word "empowerment," but in his own way Henry was saying, "You've made Charles a puppet. You don't empower him to be or do anything."

Henry then asked, "Where are company books?" They were in a safe in my office. He named other items, all of which were under my close supervision.

"Paul think he can do everything in company better than anybody else," Henry concluded. I had never managed a large company before and didn't know how to lead it effectively.

I asked, "What do I need to do?"

He replied, "Learn to delegate."

After Henry flew home, I called in the right people and delegated all the accounting, corporate books, etc. to them. Then I called Charles in and said, " You are now in charge of developing the sales training manuals. If you need ideas, let me know, but otherwise, it's your baby."

I learned that you can delegate a job without abdicating authority and that you need to inspect what you expect. My time with the old Chinese businessman was a turning point in my business, but I would have missed it all had I made the wrong choice.

The little choices that we encounter on a daily basis may seem trivial, but they also hold the greatest potential for our future. Make the right choices!

If You Don't Have Discipline, You Don't Have Anything

Why discipline is paramount to your success

A long-time friend, Bernard Rapoport, used to play tennis every morning from 6:30-7:15 on my court. I could set my watch by him. Afterwards he drove directly to his office where he showered, dressed, and was working before 8 a.m.

One day, as he was hurrying to his car, I asked him, "Why are you so regimented? Why don't you relax a little?"

He replied, "If you don't have discipline, you don't have anything!" I was taken aback, but what he said is exactly right—if you don't have discipline, you don't have anything!

Discipline is a must-have

Some things in life would be good to have, like a raise, a better boss, or a Ph.D. Then there are things you must have, like food, water, and air. *Discipline ranks in the must-have category!*

Why? If you don't have discipline, no plan can possibly succeed. Having the discipline to follow through is what brings great plans to pass.

The great inventor, Thomas Edison, explained that the vast majority of his inventions were someone else's. He just finished what others started! Interestingly, while in school, Edison was told he was "too stupid to learn anything"!

> "It is one thing to praise discipline, and another to submit to it."
>
> Cervantes

I was fortunate to be taught discipline as a young man, learning to work, be on time, finish what I started, be dependable, organized, and to save a part of all I earned. As a result, I had more money saved at age 16 than any other teenager I knew! I started this practice at age six and have continued it to this day.

Discipline is the training that produces specific desired patterns of behavior, intended habits, and the attitudes that lead to successful performance in life. In short, discipline is what you need to get you to where you want to go.

The components of discipline

Discipline isn't somewhere waiting to be discovered … it is created. By following the five components of discipline, you will create the discipline you want and need:

#1 Firm Values

Believe in what you are doing. That will affect your choices, decisions, and actions. Because I believe in what I'm doing, I don't have an ounce of worry, doubt, or insecurity.

You might need to overcome your habits, environment, or personality to fully believe in something, but deciding to do so is the first step.

#2 Setting Challenging Goals

Each of us has dreams and ambitions, as well as the ability to overcome the challenges we might face. We need the discipline of setting and reaching our goals.

Bret Miller wanted to become a doctor. Although he was from a poor family and could not afford the tuition, he refused to lay down his dream and pursued it with everything within him. He did what it took to get into school, to stay in school, and then to graduate. Today he is a successful orthopedic surgeon.

By taking personal responsibility, Bret was saying, "I have a dream within me that will become a reality if I do my part to get there."

#3 Clear priorities

You have to take the right actions to get the right results. But before you can take the right actions, you must have clearly defined priorities.

Clarify your goal. What is it exactly that you want to accomplish? When you know precisely where you are going, you can take the right actions ... which will lead you to the right results!

In addition, by keeping up the right actions for the right reasons, you are more likely to maintain the discipline you need to accomplish your goals.

The ant, for instance, is so small and carries a seemingly insignificant spec of mortar or food. Yet I have seen ants build or destroy structures of enormous proportions. Ants stay at a single task until it is complete.

#4 Persistence

Sheer persistence has enabled people to claim great accomplishments. Best-selling author and friend, Dick Francis, sits down at the same time every day to write, "whether I feel like it or not." His track record of persistence speaks for itself: over 30 best-selling books, a new book every year, a personal relationship with the Royal family in England, and more.

And what about Michael Jordan? Considered by many to be the best basketball player of all time, he was turned down by his high school

> "Perseverance is based on two components: effort and desire."
>
> Cal Ripken, Jr.

basketball coach. Jordan wisely asked, "What do I need to do to get on the team?" The coach simply told him to master the basics. So, Jordan went home and practiced his shooting, dribbling, and passing hour after hour, and the rest is history.

You can do and be anything—if you keep at it.

#5 Personal Inspiration

Creating your own inspiration will truly motivate you. Though 57 different companies rejected me before I finally got my first job selling insurance, I kept trying. I knew I would eventually be hired.

From there, I worked hard. I set goals. Eventually I became the best salesman in that company and every other insurance company I worked for.

The more discipline you have, the more "luck" some people will say you have. You know better. I believe you reap what you sow. Good results are not accidents!

Where the rubber meets the road

Bad habits require no discipline, but the habits you want require discipline. Sadly, most people perform in keeping with their own low expectations. They could be or do absolutely anything they dreamed of, so why settle for less?

I believe they don't know what their mission is in life, they don't have a personal relationship with God, and they don't comprehend the hidden power of discipline.

> "The greatest composer does not sit down to work because he is inspired, but becomes inspired because he is working."
>
> Earnest Newman

When Bernard Rapoport told me at precisely 7:15 a.m., "If you don't have discipline, you don't have anything," he was right. In his 80s now, Bernard recently bought another company after selling his first company for millions of dollars. His wife said to me, "Why stop him? It will add 10 years to his life."

Once discipline gets in your system, it becomes a natural part of all you do. That's important, because if you have discipline, you can have anything!

The Importance of Priorities

Because you live according to your priorities

When I was young, my dad took me to a foundry where they made patterns to produce large machinery parts out of iron. It was everything I did NOT want to do, and though I didn't have an established list of priorities at the time, I knew in my heart I could never work in a place like that.

Some people take any job and try to make it work, while others complain, but do nothing to change. I knew as a young teenager that somewhere there was a career that would fit me perfectly. Until then, I refused to commit to something I would dislike.

I learned that priorities protect me from making unwise decisions, point me in the right direction, *and* ensure that I get there as quickly as possible.

Priorities are to be set, then kept

Your time is subservient to your priorities, because what you choose to do, you make time to do. As Byron Weathersbee, President of Legacy Family Ministries, wisely states, "You don't even need to know what your priorities are. You just do them!"

Knowing your priorities, however, is clearly the best option. When people have poorly defined priorities, they have difficulty saying "no," even when they don't want to do something. If I'm asked to do something that goes against my priorities, I decline without giving it much thought.

Here are my priorities in order of importance:

1. God: accomplishing His will and deepening my personal relationship with Him

2. My wife: loving, protecting, nurturing, guiding, serving, and providing for her

3. My family: loving, training, encouraging, and leading by example

4. My personal health and fitness: staying in shape and eating the right foods

5. Business: being a good steward with what I have while delegating to capable individuals

> People who have a hard time saying "no" have poorly defined priorities.

The challenge is keeping all five balanced at the same time. I've also learned that *all priorities are not equal.* The average husband would say his family is a priority, but most fathers spend between 30 seconds and a few minutes of quality time with their children each day. No wonder children are more highly influenced by their peers than by their parents.

Do these men just have their priorities out of order? I believe their priorities are just fine … they simply aren't keeping them.

How to keep your priorities

Priorities are only good when they are kept. For my priorities to become a reality, I must:

1. write down my priorities
2. decide that I will keep my priorities (commit)
3. post my priorities in highly visible places
4. start with a very small action that daily reinforces my priorities
5. learn to do that small action right away

6. refuse to go to bed until I have done what I intended to do
7. create a visible checklist or tracking system
8. find an accountability partner (someone I can be honest with who will be honest with me)
9. have picture reminders
10. concentrate on the benefits
11. review regularly to see if I am on target
12. choose to never make excuses
13. craft a personal mission statement (explained below)

If one of your priorities is to spend time each day with your children, then you must take some action steps. Turn off the TV, help them with their homework, work on something in the garage together, etc. By not letting distractions get in your way you will be able to keep this important priority.

> Most people have priorities—the problem is they don't keep them.

The effort involved in making and keeping priorities is really a life-long commitment. Bottom line, *priorities are habits*. And like any good habit, it takes time for them to be established in your conscious and subconscious mind. Action naturally follows.

What is *your* life mission statement?
One of the most significant elements in keeping your priorities is the creation of a personal mission statement that serves to support your priorities.

A mission statement will also help insure that your priorities are the right priorities. My parents told me, "Do what you do for the right reasons and keep your priorities straight."

People sometime confuse a life's mission statement with a philosophy for living. The difference is this:

Life's mission statement: your reason for doing what you want to do in life (*why you will do it*).

Philosophy for living: your approach to what you want to do in life *(how you will do it).*

For example, my top priority is also my first mission statement and has to do with my relationship with God. Out of that relationship comes one of my philosophies for living: financial stewardship with what God has entrusted to me.

Some ask, "Which comes first, priorities or a mission statement?" I would say they form at the same time. Most people find their life mission statement is very similar to their priorities.

I recommend individuals sit down and carefully form a life mission statement. This enables them to keep their established priorities and may even reveal something missing in their lives.

How to write your own mission statement

Writing a life mission statement is quite simple. You begin by writing out your priorities in descending order, and then answering the question, "What do I want to accomplish in life by keeping my priorities?" Or, "Why do I have these priorities?"

> "You hit no higher than you aim."
>
> Bob Richards,
> pole vault gold
> medalist in the 1952
> and 1956 Olympics

What you write should be your overall goal for doing what you do. If one of your priorities is to help people less fortunate than you, your mission statement should outline the reason for wanting to do that. If you are married and/or have children, ask yourself why you are making your spouse and/or your children a priority.

This will reveal your heart or motive behind your actions and further impress upon your mind why your priorities are so important. If your priorities are written down, this crystallizes your thinking and helps you focus on your future.

You can keep improving on your mission statement as time goes by. By fine-tuning it, you are simultaneously fine-tuning your overall life's direction.

Lastly, a mission statement is not an exercise to complete and then forget. Keep it handy and it will benefit you greatly, including:

1. providing you with inspiration, direction, focus, and consistency in all your actions

2. keeping you on track toward your goals

3. increasing both your personal effectiveness and leadership because you know where you are going and your purpose for achieving your goals

4. serving as a motivator and a tool for simplifying your life and reducing your stress

5. improving your ability to evaluate your goals and make quick, positive decisions

Each of us fulfills our own self-definitions, simply because what we say greatly affects what we actually become. When we have carefully evaluated our priorities and mission statements and written them down, then we have a good definition from which to base our hopes, goals, and dreams.

Making them into reality is the next step, but with your priorities and mission statement in place, there is nothing to stop you!

My Word Is My Bond

Why keeping your word is absolutely invaluable

An employee once came into my office and confided in me, "I don't think I have much longer to live. Would you please make sure my wife is taken care of?"

Nothing was wrong with him physically, but for some reason he didn't think he would live much longer. My immediate response was, "Then let's get a life-insurance policy on you." He thought I was joking, but he went ahead and got a policy. Less than 90 days later he was dead from a brain aneurysm!

Though my company had taken out the life-insurance policy, I had made his wife the beneficiary. In addition, I paid her half of her husband's regular salary for 17 years until she qualified for social security funds. I also had someone manage her insurance money so she could continue with her same lifestyle.

> The only thing more costly than keeping your word is not keeping your word.

Why all the effort and expense even though I wasn't legally bound? I had told my friend that I would take care of his wife and I kept my word because *my word is my bond.*

Get it in ink!

Every year people become less trusting and more suspicious. The increase in the size of contracts and in the number of lawyers required to explain them is indicative of that lack of trust. Whether it is from greed, dishonesty, or from being abused and mistreated, it is sad to see the way the world has changed.

I was not raised that way. It was pounded into my head to be honest, which always included being:

1. dependable
2. accountable
3. reliable
4. credible

I was taught that you should say what you mean and mean what you say, and that whether you said it or put it in writing, you could be trusted to do what you agreed to do. As a result, I believe God has honored me, protected me, and blessed me.

Keeping your word has its perks

Though lawyers call me crazy, I continue "signing" deals with a handshake. Not long ago I saw a housing complex for sale. It turned out the owner's husband was sick in the hospital and they didn't know what to do and didn't know how to manage the money if the property did sell. I advised her to give the complex to a local seminary and the seminary would in turn support her and her husband for the rest of their lives.

She agreed to do it, which solved their financial problems, but it meant that I couldn't buy the property. Then six months later the seminary called and asked if I would be interested in buying a housing complex they had recently been given, not knowing it was the same complex! I bought it by borrowing

> "Who steals my purse steals trash ... but he that filches from me my good name robes me of that which not enriches him, and makes me poor indeed."
>
> Shakespeare's Othello

100 percent of the money back from the seminary, with 2 extra points of interest, and a year later sold the complex for 60 percent more than I paid for it!

People don't usually buy anything without seeing it, but I've sold 70-80 percent of my antique cars by telling the person on the end of the phone to "take my word for it," and they haven't been disappointed.

The value of keeping your word

People believe and trust me because I keep my word. I don't just say it; I actually do what I say I will do.

Businessman and president of Faith@Work ministries Bill Nix, defines trust as "the foundation on which our relationships are built. Promise keeping is the adhesive, the substance of our character that prevents the foundation of trust from cracking." He reports that discrimination lawsuits in the workplace have increased by 2,200 percent since 1980!

> Keeping your word to your children **is** the most important business deal possible.

If people forget a promise they've made, I do not believe they are excused from keeping their word. Either they should not make a promise they won't keep, or they should write it down for safekeeping. People don't usually break just one promise.

I update my will regularly, writing in the promises I have made to certain people and marking off promises I have fulfilled. Not only is my word my bond, but it is also a measurement of me as an individual. If I don't keep my word, then my advice, encouragement, counsel, etc. are all suspect.

What's more, I recognize that to accomplish anything in life, I need other people. If I break my promises, there is no possible way I will reach my goals.

During a long road trip a friend and I happened to meet seven young people who all dreamed of going to college. I told each one that I would help and asked them to write me a letter in 30 days telling me what they planned to do with their degrees. Believe it or not, only one wrote me! This young lady got her wish (I put her through college), but I never understood why the other six never took me up on my offer!

Our "yes" should mean "yes" and our "no" mean "no." Trust, respect, increased business, growth, peace of mind, and much more come as a result. Imagine what the world would be like if we all kept our word!

Keeping my word—for good

When people promise me something, I believe what they say and make a note to remind them in a couple weeks of their promise. If they don't plan to follow through, I erase it from my mind. Though disappointed, their unfulfilled promise rests in their hands, so I release them and do not hold it against them.

> "Keep your promises, even if others fail in keeping the promises they make to you."
>
> Bill Nix

There was a time when it seemed like everyone and everything was against me. The insurance company I worked for went from boom to bust in one weekend when the owners walked away, taking every dollar and piece of equipment with them. I could have walked away as well, but I chose to stay behind and put the pieces back together.

I used over a million of my own hard-earned dollars to fix what I had not broken. I realized that all the money in the world could never be more valuable than my word—*because my word is my bond.*

In the end, I will always come out far ahead.

Integrity: It's All You Are

If all you have is integrity, you have more than enough.

At every building's base is a foundation. Without it, rain, wind, and weather would bring the structure to the ground. Similarly, on a personal level, it is not difficult to distinguish who has built his or her life on a foundation of integrity and who has not.

Integrity is where it all begins

Integrity is not what you imagine or wish it to be. It is real and measurable and includes such traits as:

- taking responsibility
- being honest
- keeping your word
- being faithful in the little things

> Do the right thing because it's the right thing to do.

You cannot pretend to have integrity. The new obstacles and opportunities you face each day will draw out what is inside you. If your foundation is one of integrity, your decisions will bear that out. If not, that too will become evident.

Years ago I was selling juice dispensers with plans to get a franchise of my own. After a month of selling, I discovered information about the company that undermined my confidence in the product and franchising possibilities. When I discussed my findings with the owner, he dismissed me as being young, inexperienced, and flat wrong.

I immediately called the individuals I had sold on the franchising potential and recommended that they get a refund since it was still within the three-month trial period. When my boss found out, he fired me on the spot, but I was on my way out the door anyway.

Integrity has its price

Money was not the deciding factor about my integrity. Even if you lose money, fame, and friendships, nothing is worth trading your integrity for. I've experienced businesses drying up instantly due to one person's lack of prudence, banks unexpectedly calling my loans in before they were due, and Christian businessmen walking away from commitments, leaving me holding the bill.

Whatever the price, integrity has a greater value. My parents taught me, ***"Do the right thing because it's the right thing to do."*** If I lost a sale by being honest, I made a bigger sale *because* of my honesty. If I gave coworkers the limelight instead of me, I gained a higher caliber of leader to manage my companies. If I lost friendships, they were not really friends after all. If I lost money by keeping my word to employees, I gained employees who stayed with me for decades!

> What is the maximum price you willl pay to keep your integrity?

Everything I ever lost by choosing integrity was really not a loss at all. Proverbs 20:21 states, *"An inheritance gained hastily at the beginning will not be blessed at the end."* Anything I gained would have been temporary at best, bringing long-term hurt in the end.

Desiring to be a person of integrity does not make you perfect. I haven't always made the right moves, but God has always forgiven me and provided an opportunity for a fresh start. Sometimes the fresh start meant rebuilding from the foundation again, but at least the foundation was there. There were times when I literally had nothing left but my integrity. It was not easy, but for my character and future, it did wonders!

Integrity has its rewards

I was working on this incredible business deal when the key decision-makers tried to force me to pay a bribe. I refused and the whole thing fell apart. I was as good as broke at that stage in my life, but I clung to my integrity. With my business venture down the drain, I chose to work for a record company in their sales and marketing division.

Two years later I launched Success Motivation Institute (SMI) with all I had: my integrity, very limited cash, and a whole lot of vision. SMI began to grow, but things were tight. I flew to New York to meet with a large business owner who liked what we were offering. He guaranteed the sale if we took out every reference to anything spiritual from our materials.

> Every time I felt the only thing I possessed was my integrity, I discovered that I still had plenty.

I replied, "Well, I guess I just missed a sale." That sale was the boost we needed to make ends meet, but undermining my integrity was not an option. I cried most of the way home.

There was a letter waiting for me upon my return; an insurance company in the Midwest wanted me to speak to the key managers in their sales department. I told them they would not have to pay me if they would let me have a few minutes to offer our sales programs to the 87 managers in attendance. They agreed, so I immediately loaded a truck with 87 of our sales courses.

My mind was made up. *I was going to sell 100 percent of those in attendance!* I also NEEDED to sell them to pay our bills. When I made the sales presentation, the atmosphere was almost electric—and I sold all 87 programs!

Charles Roth, author of more than 27 books on selling, happened to be an invited guest that day. He later wrote in one of his books that my sales presentation was the best he had ever witnessed in his entire life.

By selling all 87 programs, we got the boost our company desperately needed. I believe God honored me for sticking to my convictions.

Since that time, SMI and many other companies that I've started have grown by leaps and bounds. With integrity as the bedrock foundation, the sky is truly the limit!

Integrity—are you bound to it?

Laws were designed to back up what we would normally do on a personal level. For example, individuals who have to be threatened with losing their driver's license or being put in jail in order to pay child support are really being controlled by the law. If they were bound by integrity, no police action would be necessary.

Similarly, businesspeople who train their sales team to be less than honest are undermining the whole basis of business and sales: trust, respect, and honor.

Does integrity bind and restrict or does it bring freedom and peace? It is constricting to those who don't want to do what is right, while it is freeing to those who recognize the benefits of integrity. Integrity, at its foundation, is an issue of the heart.

In your journey of life, if you ever find yourself with nothing left but your integrity, you have more than enough to start again!

Philosophy for Living
Why a philosophy for living is necessary for life

A financial advisor once said people spend more time planning for their next summer vacation than they do making financial preparation for the futures. The reason for this statistic is not that people don't care about their future, their children, or their financial well being; it is that they don't have a philosophy for living.

Having a reason for what you do, whether it is financial in nature or not, is half the battle towards getting something done. Drafting your own philosophy for living will help ensure that you actually do what you want and need to do.

Discovering your philosophy for living
Everyone is different, but as for me, I am a goal-setter. This means I have a goal-awareness, a goal-setting consciousness, a goal-setting behavior, and a goal-setting habit. A long time ago I realized that the only way I could be sure to achieve the goals that were important to me would be to plan ahead for them. Without planning, goals and purposes get pushed aside by circumstances and schedules.

At the basis of my goals lies a spiritual foundation: my relationship with Jesus Christ and my dependence on God. From that I built outward, and as I worked to clarify my thinking about my goals, I formulated a five-point philosophy for living.

These five points do not constitute an elaborate grid by which I measure my goals. Instead, each is a single aspect or approach to life that I hold very dear. Combined together, they form a philosophy for living that ensures I live life as I want to and need to.

My philosophy for living ties into my goal-setting nature, but is just as easily applicable to another person's temperament. Whatever it is that brings out the best in you, formulate a philosophy for living that guarantees you will get to where you hope to go.

The five points from my philosophy for living are as follows:

Point #1 A positive attitude

I have a positive attitude and was taught that the glass is half-full, not half-empty. I've taken that principle and expanded it so that I see the glass as full, even if it isn't, and then I seek ways to make it overflow.

Someone told me that what we are able to accomplish in life is 12 percent education and skill and 87 percent attitude and ability to communicate. I've come to see that this is 100 percent true, further impressing on me the belief that the power of a positive attitude is unlimited.

Point #2 No worry

I do not worry and haven't for many years. Instead of worry diluting my strengths and abilities, I am filled with peace and hope.

Quite simply, worry has no gain. Not worrying should be part of everyone's philosophy for living.

Point #3 Peace and contentment

I have learned to be happy every day because every day is new. Realistically, I know that all sunshine makes a desert, which means there will be different seasons, changes, storms, rain, growth, pruning, etc. Some days will feel great, others will feel lousy, and some will be up, while others will be down. The secret is to have peace and contentment regardless of what situation I am in.

Point #4 Strength and power to achieve

I see myself as an entrepreneur and a risk-taker who is courageous, bold, assertive, and willing to attempt new ideas and seek new paths. My potential to achieve is unlimited, backed by the power of Christ. I know if I seek His will and make Him my constant companion and partner that He will give me strength and power to believe. After all, His Word boldly proclaims, *"I can do all things through Christ who strengthens me"* (Philippians 4:13).

Point #5 Stewardship

Obviously, everything belongs to God by right of creation. Out of His love for me, He lets me use some of His riches. Because I have committed my life to Christ and put Him on the throne of my life (meaning He is in control), I know that what I do and achieve is because of Him.

Even the joy and pleasure I find in giving and sharing are made possible because of Him. But God, being the perfect steward, honors our acts of stewardship by blessing us more in return. He said, *"Give, and it will be given to you: good measure, pressed down, shaken together, and running over will be put into your bosom. For with the same measure that you use, it will be measured back to you"* (Luke 6:38). And *that* is just what He does!

What is your philosophy for living?

Every person should have a philosophy of living. But forming such a philosophy is not enough. It must be written down. I am a strong believer in writing things down because writing crystallizes thought (and forces you to think out your ideas more clearly) and crystallized thinking motivates positive action.

Take time to write out your personal philosophy for living. It may be similar to mine or another you've seen, or it may be entirely different. At its core, it must express your uniqueness and reflect all of the important areas of your life.

Then when you have it written down, hone the words until you feel it accurately reflects your inner desires. When it is complete, print it out and place your philosophy for living in an easily accessible location. You will need to refer to it regularly until it becomes second nature for you, permeating your thoughts and actions.

After all, isn't it comforting to know where you are going and that you will eventually get there? Having a philosophy for living will not only accomplishes that for you, but it will bring far greater long and short-term rewards than the best summer vacation ever could!

Start living your philosophy for life today!

Forgiveness Brings Freedom
And it's good for you!

F orgiveness is incredible! It is absolutely freeing and exhilarating. If you are the one being forgiven, you know it feels good. Forgiving others, however, doesn't always feel so good.

Honestly, it is hard to forgive someone who has wronged you ... until you realize that until you do you are only hurting yourself!

I have an I-will-forgive-you-regardless-of-what-you-do-to-me mentality. It has taken a while to gain this mentality, but the rewards are incalculable!

Forgiveness has its price
Those who have been hurt badly and respond, "I will die first before I forgive you!" usually do! There are many bitter men and women who are intent on taking their hurts to the grave. Sadly, they often die prematurely from the effects of holding resentment, anger, and unforgiveness inside.

We have all known people who remember a hurtful event like it was yesterday, even though it happened 5, 10, or even 50 years ago. Don't they know their unforgiveness is afflicting them and everyone around them?

They refuse to forgive because forgiveness requires them to die to their "right" to be angry. Forgiveness extols a price, death to something, and that usually involves pain.

> The price of forgiveness is always less than the price of unforgiveness.

In fact, if there were no price to pay in forgiving each other, then it would not be forgiveness at all! But despite the price that forgiveness requires, the price of unforgiveness is greater! People who never forgive after 50 years have effectively been held captive for just as long, stuck in a jail they made for themselves. Their emotions, creativity, peace, joy, hope, dreams, laughter, happiness have all been minimized by their unforgiveness.

The results of forgiveness are the opposite: maximized creativity, peace, joy, and freedom. Forgiveness will always be our choice, but for me, it has always been a "no brainer" choice.

The journey of forgiveness

I grew up between to polar opposites. My mom would forgive everyone and my father would forgive no one. I had to choose which example I would follow.

One evening when I was young, my mother had prepared a delicious dinner, working most of the day to get it just right. When my father came home, he was in a bad mood, so he dumped his plate of food in his napkin and threw it out the back door!

I couldn't believe my eyes. When I asked her why she didn't throw a skillet at him, she said, "I've been married to him for 20 years and have always turned the other cheek." Then she added, referring to Matthew 18:22, "I have a long way to go until I reach *'seventy times seven.'*" I never forgot what she said.

> Forgiveness doesn't just happen. It is an act of the will.

My mother chose to forgive and it brought her such peace and joy that it bubbled out of her life. My father simply chose not to forgive; no matter how hard or awkward it made life for him or our family. I believe his attitudes were habits he learned as a young man in Germany, and though I don't excuse his actions, it helps me understand him a little better.

Faced with two options, I made the conscious decision to be a forgiving person no matter what. That decision has brought sanity where insanity reigns, love where there are feelings of hate, and peace where there could be war.

Forgiveness is a journey that brings everyone to the same pivotal spot: the cross of Jesus Christ.

The ultimate example of forgiveness

At the cross, Jesus died for sins He did not commit. He chose to die, out of obedience to God, for our sins so that we could be forgiven and have our relationship with God restored.

We did nothing to deserve His forgiveness, but the necessary price for sin (*"the wages of sin is death"* Romans 6:23) was paid, thus making our forgiveness legitimate.

Jesus paid the price for everyone, which means our sins don't have to be held against us forever! If we confess our sins, He says He will forgive us (1 John 1:9).

By rejecting Christ's offer for forgiveness, we reject the price He paid on the cross. But if we choose to accept His forgiveness, then we also choose to forgive the actions of others toward us. That is part of the package deal, because, *"If you do not forgive men their trespasses, neither will your Father forgive your trespasses"* (Matthew 6:15).

What this means is that Christians should be the most joyful, peaceful, happy, loving, and forgiving people on the planet!

Learning how to forgive

Forgiveness is first a choice and then an action. Sometimes a lot of forgiveness is required, sometimes only a little. I set no limits on the forgiveness that I give to others. (God did not put a limit on me.) Practically speaking, I could never figure out why people would rather have ulcers, heart attacks, emotional problems, or mental problems simply because they refused to forgive. I will forgive everyone because

I refuse to settle for anything less than the benefits that come from forgiveness!

If you are having trouble forgiving, these are seven helpful steps:

Step #1 Acknowledge that you have been hurt.

Step #2 Recognize that your sin against God is far greater than the worst thing any human could do to you.

Step #3 Choose outright to forgive the other person(s).

Step #4 Accept your rightful share of the conflict, if appropriate.

Step #5 Try to communicate and clear the air, with hopes of restoration.

Step #6 If nothing changes, release the person(s) and the hurt.

Step #7 Move on.

Throughout this process, I pray for the person(s) who hurt me because I find it difficult to be upset with people when I am praying for them. Restoration rests in the hands of the offending party so I leave it up to them to instigate. That is their responsibility, not mine. My responsibility is to forgive. I pray for them regularly and wish them the best, but when I move on, I don't look back.

Forgiveness is for your benefit!

Unforgiveness brings bondage, while forgiveness brings freedom. Some who hurt me have died as a result of their actions, while others continued on with no apparent change. I focus on forgiving them and living life free from the hurt and pain that I know they are experiencing. Those who offend have usually been offended, but I don't want to be part of that cycle.

People who think forgiveness is for the weak, the cowardly, and the spineless have obviously never forgiven anyone. Forgiveness requires guts, determination, perseverance, courage, and love. Forgiveness is not pretending something never happened. Forgiveness is choosing to forgive AFTER you have held the other person(s) accountable and dealt honestly with your own hurt.

If you simply act as if it never happened, then you are making God an accomplice in the wrongful action. God's desire is that you walk free and live whole, not be a doormat to be stepped on, run over, scraped up, and abused.

If you choose not to forgive, the hurt has an uncanny way of eating away at your heart and mind. I once heard that Leonardo DeVinci, as he was painting the famous Last Supper, painted the face of his enemy as the face for Judas. While it was tempting to immortalize his enemy in his art, something strange happened—he couldn't finish the picture of Christ until he forgave his enemy. The very night he erased his enemy's face was the same night that he finished the face of Christ. Forgiveness unlocked his full potential.

Some people don't have a problem forgiving others; they struggle with forgiving themselves. If we first accept the forgiveness of God, then we have every right to forgive ourselves.

Long-term benefits of forgiveness

The act of choosing to forgive is not easy at the moment of hurt and pain, but in the long run, it is the only way to go. Though getting mad, acting hateful, and being unforgiving comes easily, it is NOT the easiest route. The easiest route brings the most benefits in the end, and that route is always the path of forgiveness.

Charlie "Tremendous" Jones once said, "Our unwillingness to forgive when we've been deeply hurt breeds self-pity and bitterness."

How true! But the reverse also holds true. By forgiving, we are training ourselves to be strong, confident, joyful, peaceful, happy, and loving. These positive attributes end up affecting every other part of our life.

Truly, forgiveness is an amazing thing!

Wait to Worry

A foolproof approach to worry-free living

There is more damage created by worrying than the actual results that manifest by worrying. This is because over 90 percent of all worries never come to pass.

I knew a man who worried about absolutely everything. The habit of worrying was so ingrained in his internal system that it had become "normal." But worrying is neither normal nor necessary.

Over the years, I have made it a deliberate point not to worry. If something happens at work or at home that would constitute a worry, I address the potential worry by saying, "I'm going to wait to worry." Then when I objectively and realistically address the issue, the "obvious" need for worrying goes away.

In fact, after applying my worry to the following 3 simple tests, I have yet to find something truly worth worrying about!

Test #1 Are all the facts on the table?

The most basic test knocks out almost every potential worry. The simply question is this: "Do I understand clearly what is being asked, needed, advised, etc.?"

If you do not have all the knowledge you need, how can you make the right decision? After you gather all the relevant data, talk with every person whose judgment on the subject you value, and read every report, then and only then can you act objectively and with the proper perspective.

At this point, the worry usually dissipates.

Test #2 Do I really want to worry about this?

For me to enjoy life, remain healthy, and be full of peace, worry cannot be part of my daily routine. What I want I must pursue, and what I don't want I must purposefully avoid.

I've seen disastrous effects from worry on the lives of people *and* their children. Here are a few of the side effects of worrying:

- **Self-doubt:** This downward spiral focuses on why things cannot be done versus why things can be done.
- **Mediocrity:** Capable people become incapable of accomplishing their intended goals.
- **Fright:** Running scared is the enemy of success, peace, contentment, happiness, joy, laughter, etc.
- **No creativity:** The freedom to be creative is squelched by worry.
- **Physical ailments:** The body reacts adversely to internal worries.
- **Wasted time:** Over 90 percent of what you worry about never comes to pass.

The bottom line is this: "Can you really gain anything by worrying?" The answer is a resounding "No!"

Test #3 Is it biblically acceptable to worry?

This is the last and final test. If a situation can make it past this test, then it is indeed truly worth worrying about. However, the Bible plainly states many different times, *"Do not worry"* (Matthew 6:34). And to do what the Bible says *not to do* is a sin, plain and simple.

> To not worry, you must break the worrying habit.

Worrying not only shows a lack of trust in God, but it flies in the face of Philippians 4:6-7, which says, *"Be anxious for nothing, but in everything by prayer and supplication, with thanksgiving, let your requests be made known to God; and the peace of God, which surpasses all understanding, will guard your hearts and minds through Christ Jesus."*

It doesn't get much plainer than that, yet people regularly choose to do the opposite, then complain about the side effects of worrying. The truth is that worry shows we don't believe the Word of God. It is technically impossible to swim up two rivers at the same time, to sit on both sides of the fence at once, or to have fear and faith in the same mind at the same time. Worry and faith are opposites.

How to win over worry

People do what they do for two reasons: to gain benefit or to avoid loss. But when it comes to worrying, an even more powerful force seems to take control: bad habits. They worry because it is a habit, and whether they learned it from their parents or mastered the art for themselves, the habit must be broken. The obvious question is "How?"

Entire books have been written on this subject, but I have found that regardless of the great information, people will continue to do what they choose to do. In short, the only way to bring about change is for them to willfully choose to change their thinking.

> "A distraught mind inevitably leads to a deteriorated body."
>
> John Edmund Haggai

The best place to start is in the Word of God. As was obvious, Test #3 left no room for worrying, but many people who know better still worry constantly. Accepting the reality that worrying is a sin is the first step, repenting (turning from it) is the second.

Follow that with a conscious effort to fill your mind with relevant truths that will equip you to withstand the habit of worrying. And while you are reading, studying, and absorbing the principles found in God's Word, be obedient to whatever it is the Holy Spirit tells you to do. He knows best and He wants you to be free from worrying even more than you do!

From there, get prepared. Many people worry simply because they are not adequately prepared for what they need to do, be, or say. Learn, study, and know the facts.

> "It isn't work; it's worry that makes people tired and frustrated."
>
> J. E. Gulick

Lastly, foster within you an attitude of positively expectancy. This permeates everything I do, regardless of the "weightiness" of a task. Granted, some decisions and problems are more important than others, and while I'm concerned about them, that is not the same as being worried. I expect good things to happen.

It would be nice if worry-free living could be bundled in a package and handed to someone, but it doesn't work that way. It is a willful choice that must be made by each individual.

Make the decision for yourself to live life worry-free. It is not only possible, but it is very enjoyable!

Laughing at Life

Because we all take life a little too seriously

Whether you think it is good, bad, or ugly, you are experiencing life. No matter what you do, things happen that you cannot manage, manipulate, predict, or prevent. That is life!

Of all the things you can control, one thing has the ability to positively impact every area in your life, including the hard times. It is your ability to laugh.

Finders keepers, losers weepers

People generally find what they are looking for. I've trained myself to look for humor in every part of life, even in seemingly humorless situations. I see humor at funerals, at church, at work, at home, etc. It's not that I'm out of touch with my emotions or have a warped mind, but I purposefully look for the humor in things.

The French have a great adage that says, "The most completely lost of all days is that in which one has not laughed."

One of my constant sources of laughter is myself. Whoever said, "If you learn to laugh at yourself, you will always have something to laugh about," was absolutely correct. If I take myself too seriously, I begin to think more and more about the negative situations around me. That allows discouragement, lack of faith, hopelessness, and bitterness to seep into my life. Instead, laughter enables me to maintain a healthy perspective.

A few years ago I took my flying partner, Gene Franklin, out in my Piper Cub. Before we took off I asked the man who looked after my plane if it was ready to fly, and he said yes.

> "If you lose the power to laugh, you lose the power to think."
> Clarence Darrow

About 10 minutes into the air my plane ran out of gas! I turned to Gene in the back seat and said with a smile, "What did you used to do in your car when you were running out of gas? Slosh the gas, right?"

I turned the plane and headed back, sloshing the tanks whenever the engine started to sputter. We were about to land when I remembered there was no gas at that airfield, so I said with a laugh, "Perhaps we can make it three more miles."

We were past empty, but by sloshing the tanks from side to side we made it those three miles. As we were making our landing, the engine quit, as did the propeller. We coasted right up to the gas tanks and ran out of momentum just 3 feet away!

The situation could have been disastrous, but stressing myself out would have just impaired my ability to think clearly. I laughed at myself for not checking the fuel gauge (it's always the pilot's responsibility to do so) and it is a lesson I know I will never forget!

Why not laugh?

There is always a reason to laugh and a reason not to laugh, but you get to choose which one you want to do. Here are five reasons why cultivating the habit of daily laughter is beneficial:

#1 Laughter is good for you

Laughing is good for your health. Numerous studies, articles, and stories have detailed how people used laughter to recover from serious illnesses. Laughter has been shown to lower blood pressure, boost the immune system, and add years to your life.

Even money is not so important that you can't laugh at its gain or loss. I've woken up to find that some of my stock investments have dropped sharply or increased dramatically. Of course I prefer the increases, but the losses make me shrug and say, "You win some, you lose some, and some you get rained out."

Stress has become the greatest single contributor to illness in the industrialized world. The mind and body really are interrelated. Laughter is good for you!

#2 Laughter is powerful

Those who know how to use humor effectively usually know how to persuade others. The ability to employ humor as a tool in defusing potentially troublesome situations is a valuable resource. Best-selling author and famous motivational speaker, Zig Ziglar, uses this approach with his audiences, telling them, "It's hard to be upset at someone when you're laughing at him."

> If you can laugh at yourself, you'll always have something to laugh at.

Laughing has the power to change your world, to make you see things in their proper perspective, and enable you to keep going, even when opposition seems insurmountable. If laughter has the power to move you, inspire you, and heal you, then it has the power to change those around you as well.

#3 Laughter is fun to be around

It is fun to be around people who laugh a lot. They are upbeat and positive, rather than discouraging and judgmental. Bill Hinson, a friend since I was 20 years old, is a master of humor. He uses humor to calm arguments, explain a delicate situation, and to make someone feel comfortable.

It is no mystery why he has held so many positions of leadership. Bill's phone calls are always encouraging and his presence lifts your spirits. When he is around, you know it, and it is always a blessing.

Laughter brightens our good times and lightens our heavy times. And since we go through life with other people, we might as well enjoy the mutual ride. Laughter is the life of the party.

#4 Laughter is a good teacher

If you are responsible for training people, especially children, then use laughter to your advantage. I heard of a father who used humor to teach his daughter a valuable lesson. She had over-packed for a short say with her cousin, and instead of lecturing her, he put his most pitiful look.

She asked, "What's wrong, Daddy?" He replied, "I thought you were going for a couple days. I didn't know you were moving out!" She laughed … and agreed.

Whatever you do, include laughter and see the results improve.

#5 Laughter is better than tears

No life is perfect, but laughter is always better than sadness, resentment, or discouragement. Since there are always two choices, choose laughter every time.

Laughing all the way home

Someone asked my wife Jane what she liked most about me. She instantly said, "He makes me laugh." Of course that made me feel good.

> "Fortune comes to those who smile."
> Japanese proverb

Marriage is a great place to foster a lifelong attitude of laughter. Whether you are married or not, you would do well to heed the advice of author, Dr. Barbara Chesser. She explains how humor helps put things into perspective, for without laughter, every flaw in our marriage partner can stand out like a sore thumb.

Here are her tips for making laughter an integral part of your marriage:

- Learn to lighten up, live a little, and laugh a lot.
- Be sensitive to differences in sense of humor.
- Consider the timing of your humor.
- Don't laugh AT someone, laugh WITH them.
- Establish your own ground rules.

Then laugh when:

- There is nothing you can do but laugh.
- One or both of you do not understand what to do next.
- One of you has an overriding urge to kill the other.
- You need to positively pre-set your mind to handle a negative situation.
- When you need a safety valve to help heal the hurts of grief.

Laughter is more than good medicine—it is the best medicine! Whatever you do, learn to laugh at life.

Love: Where Success Begins

Because everything of value must start somewhere

When I was a boy, I saw love in action and learned quickly that it came in many different forms.

- My brother Carl loved me by the way he fought off three bullies when I was just 15 years old and small for my age.
- My sister Elizabeth loved me by always having a listening ear and a kind word for me.
- My father loved me by the way he trained me, disciplined me, and spent time with me.
- My mother loved me by demonstrating how to forgive, how to communicate, and how to know God.
- My teachers loved me by giving me a lot of their time.

Having love did not make life perfect. I had plenty of hurts and disappointments, not to mention many setbacks and losses, but in the midst of the realities of life, love always seemed to blossom. That is because love cannot be held captive by our thoughts, emotions, fears, or outside limitations.

The greatest commandments of all time

We are often reminded that Jesus said there was no greater commandment than to *"love the LORD your God with all your heart,*

> Love brings unstoppable freedom when we learn to love as God intended.

with all your soul, with all your mind, and with all your strength" and to *"love your neighbor as yourself"* (Mark 12:30-31).

But we are not as often told that Jesus later added, *"A new commandment I give to you, that you love one another; as I have loved you, that you also love one another"* (John 13:34). That changes things considerably! Here is a sampling of the ways that Jesus showed His love for us:

- He stopped to talk with the lowest of the low.
- He dispensed justice wherever He went.
- He healed the social outcasts.
- He cared for the poor.
- He gave up His will.
- He allowed His body to be beaten for our sake.
- He died on the cross for our sins while we were still sinners.

Loving others to the extent that He loved us is impossible, but that is the point! *We cannot do it on our own—we need Him!* And unless we have His love in our hearts, there is no way we can love others wholly, purely, or adequately.

> Love is long-term thinking. All else is short-term, if even that.

What exactly is love?

What is love? Here is the best definition of love that I have ever found: *"Love suffers long and is kind; love does not envy; love does not parade itself, is not puffed up; does not behave rudely, does not seek its own, is not provoked, thinks no evil; does not rejoice in iniquity, but rejoices in the truth; bears all things, believes all things, hopes all things, endures all things. Love never fails"* (1 Corinthians 13:4-8).

That is love.

How we practically show God's love comes in many different forms. My mother, for example, was like a magnet. Her love for others drew people to her like children to free ice cream.

Love also comes in the form of discipline. My dad gave me plenty of that, and I love him for it. If my dad had not disciplined me, I would not be the man I am today.

Sacrifice is also love in action. I have friends who sacrificially give of their time, talents, and money toward charities that are helping the homeless, hungry, and poor.

Our love should focus in three different directions: toward God, toward ourselves, and toward others.

#1 What does it mean to "love God"?

To love God is to obey Him. As we love Him with everything within us, He has an amazing way of pouring back into us. Here are just two of His many promises:

• *Eye has not seen, nor ear heard, nor have entered into the heart of man the things which God has prepared for those who love Him* (1 Corinthians 2:9).

• *Neither death nor life, nor angels nor principalities nor powers, nor things present nor things to come, nor height nor depth, nor any other created thing, shall be able to separate us from the love of God which is in Christ Jesus our Lord* (Romans 8:38-39).

#2 What does it mean to "love yourself"?

Loving God and accepting that He loves you are the foundations for loving yourself and for experiencing self-confidence and self-esteem. Loving self is not the same as being self-centered or egotistic.

Although I have always believed that I have every right to succeed, I do not believe the world owes me anything. The "everybody owes me" attitude in our society is partly the result of having no love for self. I act wisely and do the necessary preparation and planning to reach my goals. ***This belief in myself is love for self in action.*** The world can be cruel at times, and although I have been wounded by close confidants, I cannot let that get in my way.

Having confidence in self gives you confidence to be inspired by the success of others. Their phenomenal growth doesn't discourage you in the slightest because you believe you have the same potential, if not more!

Love includes self-discipline, taking responsibility, and the realization that we have a part to play in our own success. If we succeed without first establishing a firm foundation, our descent back into reality will be more painful than if we had fallen from a more lowly prior condition.

Love for self along with a firm foundation prepares us for greatness.

#3   What does it mean to "love your neighbor"?

The foundation for loving our neighbor is comprised of two parts: a proper love of self and a desire to love others as Christ loved us. And since a "neighbor" is every person, regardless of race, gender, or age, we get to love everyone!

I've made it a habit to show love to people by noticing them, listening to them, asking them questions, and discovering their interests. I make it a point to always be real, show respect, treat them as I would like to be treated, focus on their strengths, and try to be an encouragement to them. Through a series of circumstances, I've even ended up hiring many of them!

I once met an elderly man who was offering some prime property for sale. A few days later I returned to buy it, but by asking a few additional questions, I discovered that the real owners of the property had gone back on their word and were refusing to give him the commission he rightly deserved.

I immediately called the owner and said the deal was off unless he agreed to pay the commission, which he reluctantly agreed to do. The $25,000 commission came at a good time for the elderly man and his wife who had no savings for retirement. I instantly made a friend that day by simply treating someone like I would like to be treated.

Why God commands us to love other people
We all have had people rip us off, hurt us, and even abuse us. Agreeing not to retaliate is good, *but God is asking us to go even further and to love them!* Why?

I believe there are three reasons:

#1 For our benefit

From God's perspective, He is more interested in our personal growth and character development than in what we do or how we look. When we love others, we are demonstrating that we are obeying God and placing our desires second to His, a sure sign of character development.

And when others do not love us, we have the chance to show what is really in our hearts. By loving those who don't love us in return, we are showing that we are different, controlled by something stronger than our own naturally selfish desires — *it shows the love of God at work in our lives.*

I remember my mother when I think of this type of love. If people hurt her, her level of love would only increase. By choosing to love others as Christ loved her, my mother was full of joy, peace, strength, hope, laughter, and a lot more.

In whatever way we show our love for God, it is for our benefit!

In addition, when we show love through our actions, God will reward us, just as Scripture says, *"But love your enemies, do good, and lend, hoping for nothing in return; and your reward will be great, and you will be sons of the Most High"* (Luke 6:35).

#2 For their benefit

Several years ago a professional person in my town confronted me in his office with a damaging yet completely false accusation. I tried in vain to communicate the actual facts, but he would hear none of it. The conversation hurt me so badly that my health was severely affected.

I decided that I would pray for him and do all I could to help him in his personal life. Instead of mentioning this individual's actions to other professional people who might know him or meet him, I chose to forgive him. (Forgiveness and love always go together.) Two years later he called me and admitted he was wrong and asked for my forgiveness.

Love *"will cover a multitude of sins"* (1 Peter 4:8) and knows no limits. Showing the love that Jesus intended will pave the way for others to know the same Love, *which is the greatest benefit of all!*

#3 For God's benefit

I believe that by loving others as Christ loved us, we are able to accomplish His purposes in our individual lives and that is definitely to His benefit.

However, His greatest desire by far is that every individual comes to know Him as his or her Lord and Savior. Scripture says, *"God so loved the world that He gave His one and only Son, that whoever believes in Him should not perish but have everlasting life"* (John 3:16). He paid the costliest of prices for us, showing us the full extent of his love.

> "Love is an act of the will, not the exercise of emotions."
>
> John Edmund Haggai

Over the years I have hired many individuals who were down on their luck. Several went on to great careers, some moved on to another job, while a few went back to their old bad habits.

Many of those who took advantage of the opportunity of a second-start have returned and asked questions about my faith. That, I believe, is how God benefits through our acts of love.

The reality of loving others

Love that is given away might not be returned—*this is a fact of life!* Jesus commanded us to love, but He did not say we would be loved in return. I do believe, however, that we always, someway, somewhere, somehow, some day will reap what we sow. However, *it is impractical to demand love from those we have loved.* Loving is simply part of our service to others.

We cannot think that everyone will love us in return. We must learn to live with some rejection, recognizing that we have been primarily and most importantly obedient to God and His Word. We can then walk in peace, *which makes what others say or do completely irrelevant!*

Love plays a vital role in your success.

We All Stand on
Level Ground

The importance of seeing others eye to eye

Whoever heard of being raised with no prejudice, no color lines, no socio-economic lines, no position lines, no gender lines, and no educational lines? Is that even possible? I would doubt it, except for the fact that I was raised this way.

My parents taught me that everyone stood on level ground, and from that one truth many other principles were driven into my formative heart and mind. Being first-generation German immigrants to the United States, their I-will-not-be-denied attitude is what enabled them to survive.

I had to rely on the same attitude when I went on my first job search. I applied to 57 different companies and was denied by every single one of them because I did not have a college education. Without asking what I could do, how motivated I was, or anything about my work ethic, they all said, "No thanks."

Life did NOT seem fair! But instead of quitting, I kept trying. I finally got a job selling insurance to black families out in the country. They considered it to be the lowest job possible.

I jumped at the opportunity because my dad had always said, "Never take a higher position without first being an apprentice." What I learned was invaluable, as were the wonderful people I met.

I went on to out-perform every salesman I laid eyes on and won every sales competition I entered. The way I see it, every company lost that did not give me an equal chance.

Similarly, if we discredit a person without giving him or her a fair chance, we lose as well. We must retrain our hearts and minds to see people as they ought to be seen. After all, there was a time when we were young, inexperienced, and denied for some unexplainable reason ourselves.

Don't look up—and don't look down.

My parents taught me to keep my eyes fixed straight ahead. That way I wouldn't think too highly of some (as if they can do no wrong) or too lowly of others (as if they can do no right). The lowest paid person deserves the same respect as the highest paid person.

A medical doctor friend of mine, Winn Henderson, once told me that he has had more than 160 different jobs. From washing windows to performing brain surgery, he has done it all, but he says, "I was just as proud doing the menial job as the 'respected' one because all honest work is valuable."

> Don't let someone else's attitude prevent you from getting what is rightfully yours!

Treating everyone as equals, however, doesn't fit well with some people, especially when it comes to skin color. When I was 18 years old, I happened to go into a restaurant in Georgia that had a U-shaped counter with a wire screen in the middle dividing the "coloreds" from the "whites."

When the waiter came to take my order, I asked, "What color are the people in the kitchen?" He said they were all black, so I said, "Well, don't you feel a little foolish eating the same food with the same forks and same plates cooked by the same cooks?"

While in the military, which had its fill of disrespectful and demeaning people, my eyes were opened to the "real world." I had grown up around Italians, Hispanics, Japanese, Germans, etc., and I thought nothing of it, but apparently others did. One of my best friends when I was a young happened to be an American of Japanese descent, so when WW II started, he and his whole family were interned.

When I found he was being forced to move, I went to his house and gave him my most prized possession: my new bicycle that I had spent months saving up money to buy. It was my way of saying, "The system is wrong, but I believe in you. You are my friend."

When I couldn't change the abuse that was taking place, I could make sure that I never did the same when I was in the position of authority. That is the beauty of the I-will-not-be-denied attitude. If you want something, go get it. *Don't let someone else's attitude inhibit you from getting what is rightfully yours!*

It comes down to choices, whether we want to believe something we've learned or not. Fortunately for me, what I was taught was also what is correct—*that we all stand on level ground.* That is one reason that I have always been able to call on anyone, anywhere, any place, at any time, with a fearless attitude and belief that I will never be rejected. I believe that the welcome mat is always out for me. Why not, since I always have the welcome mat out for others!

Imagine what the world would be like if we lived out the belief that we all stand on level ground!

Now *that* is success!

The Journey of Prayer

You'll never be the same!

When I became a father at age 21, I began to pray in earnest. The fact that I was suddenly responsible for something far more important than any job or position I had ever held was a compelling motivation!

The truth is prayer had always seemed dry, boring, and ineffective, but the more I prayed, the more I discovered about life, about God, and about myself—*and it was far from what I had first imagined!*

Prayer is communicating with God, talking to Him, and having Him talk back to me. Having an open line of communication between God and myself meant I had to overcome two very real obstacles in my way: barriers and distractions.

#1 Barriers

The primary barrier that keeps me from communicating with God is sin. (Sin is simply doing what God says not to do.) I must repent before I can communicate with God, not because He doesn't love me and doesn't want to talk with me, but because He is Holy—and holiness and sin do not mix! Isaiah 59:2 says, ("*...your iniquities have separated you from your God; and your sins have hidden His face from you, so that He will not hear.*")

> Prayer is all about a long-term relationship between God and you.

#2 *Distractions*

Distractions are not usually sins, but are such basic things as being overly tired, sleeping too long, and interruptions (children, phones, TV, music, etc.). They are subtle, minor, and of seemingly little consequence, yet they are effective communication blocks.

For most of us, the primary distraction is our own lack of discipline. I have trained myself to pray every morning for an hour before I get out of bed because I am able to focus on my prayers without pondering the concerns of the day. It also prepares me for the decisions, opportunities, and challenges that are sure to come.

Why do I pray?

Here are 5 reasons why prayer is so important to me:

#1 *I love to pray.*

If you stop and think about it, talking with the Creator of the universe is no small matter, and that He would want to communicate on a personal level with me is almost incomprehensible! And the more I pray, the closer we get in our relationship. (This is only natural, since the more I communicate with my wife, the more we know each other.)

#2 *I'm not in control.*

The fact of the matter is that *I am never in complete control.* I can control my attitude, my spending habits, and my medication, but there is no way I can control the weather, the stock market, or the actions of other people.

Several years ago my oldest daughter Janna was involved in a car accident. Something fell off the seat and she leaned over to retrieve it. She looked up just in time to put on the brakes before she crashed into a tree. Though the car was damaged, thankfully she escaped without any serious injury.

God is the only one in control, so I pray that He will orchestrate events on my behalf.

#3 I need help.

I love to help people, but I recognize that without God's assistance, my efforts are far from what they could be. For instance, my friend Dr. J. Clifton "Clif" Williams had Hodgkin's disease and the doctors had given him just months to live, so he had put his estate in order and prepared his family for the inevitable.

When I first walked into his hospital room, I shared thoughts about Clif's wife, Jan, and their two children, Eric and Lynn, ages six and eight. Then I brazenly said, "If you seriously want to live, then you need to change your attitude and start visualizing life as if you were going to live and not die! Get an attitude of positive expectancy for life, such as visualizing your kids at their grammar school, high school, and college graduations. What will you be wearing? Where will you go out to eat afterwards?"

I continued, "Until your children leave home for college, what will you do to impress your Christian values on them? Where will you go for family vacations? What have you and Jan always wanted to do together as a family?"

> Through prayer, we willl not change God in any way; we pray and we are changed ourselves.

"If you want to see tomorrow," I concluded, "then you need to bring the future into present focus through a positive attitude, visualization, and setting goals."

With Clif's faith in God, his wife's fervent prayers, the love from his friends and family, and his ability to envision a healthy future, his health was positively affected. Even though he was sick for a couple years—lymph glands removed, blood transfusions, and diet changes—he slowly and gradually regained his strength. That was almost 30 years ago!

#4 I want things to change.

Prayer does indeed change things, but the majority of the change takes place in me. At times when I pray for certain people who have been malicious in their comments or actions toward me, I am the one who ends up changing (forgiving, but not excusing them).

I've loaned money to people who then refused to repay what they owed. Several times during prayer I was impressed to forgive the debt. God uses what has damaged me to bring freedom, blessing, and peace into my life. Much of what I've gone through was for one reason: God wanting to perfect me. Praying that a hard circumstance will go away might not be to your benefit. Instead, pray for His will to be done—then go with the flow.

#5 *I need to do His will*

Jesus prayed, *"Not My will, but Yours be done"* (Luke 22:42). His purpose was to accomplish God's will. I have the same purpose, *as does every Christian*, which means my prayers ought to be for what He has for me to do, not for my own selfish desires.

Several years ago I wanted to set up a program to help the economically disadvantaged youth in my town go to college. In prayer God revealed to me an innovative way to make the vision into a reality. As a result, our family set up the *Passport to Success Foundation* as the financial vehicle to make this possible.

This inspired other Waco families to start their own programs, including the MAC Grant Foundation, the Rapoport Foundation, and the Clifton Robinson Foundation. The combined efforts of these foundations have already helped over a thousand disadvantaged youth in our county go to college!

The reality of prayer

It didn't take much time in prayer before I discovered another vital ingredient of prayer: obedience. When He speaks, we are to obey, even if it doesn't make sense.

A friend told me of a young missionary woman who was traveling alone in Bangladesh. As she stepped off a bus, a family begging for bus fare back to their hometown approached her. The young lady quickly prayed and felt like God was telling her to give them all she had and to keep only a few dollars. She obeyed, and before she had taken more than 20 steps, a thief wielding a knife demanded her money. She almost laughed as she gave him all she had—just the few dollars!

Obedience protects, directs, and catapults us to heights we could never have imagined otherwise.

What makes prayer effective

For prayer to be effective, faith is required. Without faith, prayer accomplishes virtually nothing ... but with faith, anything is possible!

One day I read *"God is love"* (1 John 4:8) and something clicked. If God is Love, then it follows that He cannot be mean, cruel, hateful, spiteful, or selfish. It is impossible! Everything He does is then based in what He is—complete and perfect love.

Tracking answers in a journal

Many years ago I began to list in my prayer journal the names of people who needed prayer along with a brief note about their needs to keep me focused. When a prayer was answered, I put the date beside it. Re-reading those answered prayers refreshes me and fills me with faith to keep praying, keep believing, and keep expecting God to move on my behalf.

In my journal are many different lists, each marked with a distinct title and colored tab. Some topics include: personal and family concerns, the ministries that are close to my heart, friends and acquaintances, and the names of people who have hurt me.

I have seen rebellious children change, marriages restored, dismal financial situations improve, and people's hard hearts melt with compassion, all as a result of steadfast, tenacious prayer.

> "Unless the vital forces of prayer are supplied by God's Word, prayer, though earnest in its urgency, is, in reality, flabby and vapid and void."
>
> E. M. Bounds

Prayer requires action

While praying, I often feel I need to do something for a person, such as mailing books, writing letters, making phone calls, postponing meetings, canceling trips, and more.

One family I met appeared to have a perfect life: good jobs, great house, fabulous children, etc. During several conversations with them, however, I found they were in financial straits and were in some denial about personal problems. I felt their dilemma came from the fact that none of them had a personal relationship with Jesus Christ.

We talked numerous times, I had an accountant help them with their finances, and I gave them several books. Months later, the father called to say the entire family had accepted Christ! It is exciting to watch as every previous problem that was a part of their life is being resolved.

He wants to answer our prayers

We must believe that God hears, that He cares, and that He acts on our behalf. That is faith. Jesus said, *"Ask, and it will be given to you; seek and you will find; knock, and it will be opened to you"* (Matthew 7:7). It takes effort to ask, seek, and knock until an answer comes.

> "God does nothing but in answer to prayer."
>
> John Wesley

Instead of an immediate answer, we often experience delay, which in turn tests the strength of our faith. I have had prayers that took many years to be answered. In fact, some of my most meaningful and encouraging answers to prayer came after several years of praying.

Does this mean that God answers every prayer I have ever prayed? Yes, I believe He does answer all my prayers, though not necessarily in the way I might want.

I find great comfort in the fact that God wants to give good things to us (Matthew 7:11). The fact is, He desires to answer our prayers—

we just need to be willing to do our part through diligent prayer, faith, and action.

Prayer allows God's power to be revealed and His plans to come to pass. Through prayer, I have experienced God's power, wisdom, favor, and creativity in my life to a degree that I could never have imagined!

As a result of prayer, my world has changed and I know I'll never be the same ... *and neither will you!*

Multiply Your Gifts and Talents

Learning to master your exponential potential

Anon-profit organization called a few years ago and asked if I would support their ministry financially. I believed in what they were doing, but I said, "No, I have a better idea."

My view has always been that giving someone a handout is never as profitable as giving someone a hand up, so I offered to pay the salary of a development director for two years who would in turn raise the funds the organization needed. They agreed, and by the time those two years had passed, the development director raised 5 to 10 times what I was paying for his salary!

> Multiplication is a mind-set before it is a reality.

When you cannot serve to the degree that those you have helped are now serving others, that is when you know you have multiplied yourself!

Multiply whatever you have

We all have different talents and abilities. Some have more, some have less, but this does not make one person better than another. Those who boast about their talents need to understand two important facts:

- First, our natural gifts are just that, gifts, and they are from God and are not self-generated.
- Second, God expects more from those who have been blessed with much.

Whatever it is that God has given us, His desire is that we use it wisely so that it multiplies.

Making multiplication commonplace

Though multiplication is taught in school, why is it so uncommon in real life? Whether it is mismanagement, pride, or lack of vision, multiplication is a seldom occurrence.

There are exceptions, however. One of the best examples of multiplication is that of the Haggai Institute. The concept of the institute's founder, John Haggai, is simple:

- Train indigenous leaders how to reach their own people with the gospel of Jesus Christ, then
- Train these Christian leaders how to equip other people for evangelism.

Since 1969, the Haggai Institute has trained over 40,000 indigenous Christian leaders in more than 160 different nations who in turn will each train on average 100 more people. This has created the largest missionary force in the world, exceeding all Christian denominations combined!

Another example of multiplication is Baylor University in Waco, Texas. In 1963 they asked if I could help raise money for their college. Instead of going on the road or phoning the alumni to raise the money, I had them mark on a map where all the past students lived. I encouraged them to make a 16-mm movie about the university, detailing the history, present stage, successful students, possible plans for the future, how much money it would cost, etc. and to use these alumni as contact points. They showed this movie around the nation while recruiting fund-raising developers and establishing campaigns to raise money.

As a result, enrollment multiplied and their 30 million-dollar endowment increased to over 700 million and soon will reach a billion, making Baylor University one of the best-endowed private colleges in North America.

Belief requires action

If I believe in something, I believe it ought to multiply. But *belief requires action for multiplication to take place.*

Nobody can go swimming without first getting into the water. I ask people who are raising funds for a charity, "Have you given to the cause for which you are trying to raise money?" Often, they have not!

Several years ago I met Inez Russell, an extremely dedicated woman whose passion is to help those who can't help themselves. With virtually no money and a handful of volunteers, she founded Friends for Life to stop abuse, neglect and exploitation through legal guardianship, money management, and independent living programs. The people she helps are unable to perform daily tasks, such as buying groceries, cleaning their homes, and managing their bills.

> Never limit yourself by what is or what is not.

After hearing her vision, I hired a development person for Friends for Life. She now has over 2,000 volunteers to take care of 3,000 elderly people and Friends for Life is ranked 11th out of thousands of charities in the United States for its overall organization and effectiveness. Her ministry is now used as a template for others throughout the nation. That is multiplication on top of multiplication!

Don't limit yourself

By focusing on what we do not have, we limit ourselves. We also limit ourselves by focusing on what we do have. My enthusiastic friend, Bill Armor, could sell saltwater to a sailor. Not relying solely on enthusiasm, he took the time to learn how to communicate, listen, and answer questions. He became president of an insurance company, the fulfillment of his life-long dream. He reached his goal because he didn't limit himself by only what he was good at.

The first insurance company I worked for would not let me hire other people, so I was limited by the hours I could work in a single day. When I took a position with another company that allowed me to recruit other salespeople, my career took off!

Multiplication may take longer than you planned. There once was a university in England partially enclosed by a stone wall. An ivy bush was planted beside the wall with hopes that the vines would grow and cover the wall, but after many years, the ivy appeared dormant. Tired of waiting, the groundskeeper decided to give it one more year to grow.

The following year the ivy began to spread rapidly over the wall. Out of curiosity, he gently dug around the plant and discovered one primary root that went directly toward a river located more than 70 feet away! All those years the ivy bush had been putting its entire effort into reaching the river. Once that was accomplished, multiplication took place at an alarming rate. Had the groundskeeper given up too quickly, multiplication would never have been realized.

Delay is part of the multiplication process. It takes time to get everything lined up, but once that occurs, watch out because things are about to erupt!

Where the exponential potential begins
To multiply is to tap into your exponential potential. The top 6 multipliers I have experienced are:

#1 Multiplier: Connecting to God
The basis of all multiplication begins in a personal relationship with Jesus Christ. He has an infinite amount of everything I need, far more than I could handle at any one time.

It's like my house having the entire outflow of Hoover Dam's hydroelectric power plant at its disposal. There is no way I will ever be able to utilize the power behind the 17 generators inside the Hoover Dam because they have the capability of supplying all the electricity needed by a city of 750,000 people!

God living in me means that I am connected to the Creator of everything. By being plugged into Him, we truly have unlimited potential to grow, to increase, and to multiply.

#2 Multiplier: Being Creative

We all have a God-given ability to be creative. Many of us have been told what we cannot do so often that we have started to believe it. Instead, we need to envision what we can do. The ability to be creative is where potential and reality connect.

#3 Multiplier: Starting Small

It is virtually impossible to get what you want by waiting for it to fall into your lap. If you are not prepared to receive it, then you are not prepared to keep it. Starting small is therefore a good idea.

Years ago I invested in some educational software to help one child. The results were so favorable that the same software was introduced to other schools, resulting in more than 5,000 schools using this educational software today. The software company is now worth millions of dollars!

#4 Multiplier: Allowing Others to Give

I allow those who work with me to give their time and expertise to charities *on company time*. The effect on my community has been phenomenal. Several of the local charities are among the best in the nation, not to mention the fact that thousands of lives are being positively impacted daily by our efforts.

#5 Multiplier: Learning to Delegate

Delegation sets the stage for multiplication. I learned this lesson many years ago and since that time have noticed a dramatic increase in my ability to dream, plan, and pursue other ideas.

#6 Multiplier: Giving it to God

Giving up something we hold dear is a price most of us are not willing to pay. As a result, we miss the exponential growth. Scripture states, *"Unless a grain of wheat falls into the ground and dies, it remains alone; but if it dies, it produces much grain"* (John 12:24).

Sometimes dreams must die before they can reach their full potential.

I've seen hundreds of boxes of fruit come from a tree that was once a small seed. Every harvest is based on seeds "dying," and though this is a cost, the harvest makes it all worthwhile.

This process of dying to self includes the faith that what you are "losing" will come back to you. I've turned down business deals I wanted desperately because I felt God didn't want me to pursue them. Another time I let someone buy the very piece of property I wanted, then a couple of months later I bought the same property for a better price!

Whatever happens, *I always come out better off.* That is the amazing effect of giving something to God and letting Him multiply it.

The final goal of multiplication

Multiplication is mathematically intended to do one thing: *continue forever.* Bringing in a lot of money, seeing a ministry grow rapidly, or watching something multiply at an exponential rate is always enjoyable, but that cannot be the ultimate goal.

In 1967, I wrote an article and then made a speech from it. I made a tape from the speech and sold a million copies. I was paid a royalty of 25 cents a piece. I took the tape and the profits and made a full-length training program from the principles outlined in the tape. Over the years, millions of dollars in royalties have come from that one program!

But I didn't stop there! I took the ongoing royalties and invested them in several foundations. Today that same money is still growing and will continue to grow indefinitely, all from an article I wrote in 1967!

The exponential potential behind multiplication is fully expressed when growth is perpetual.

Isn't that what success is all about?

It's All His by Right of Creation

Discovering the joy and responsibility of stewardship

When I fly over a city, I often think of the courthouse below with its records of who owns which parcel of land. People think they own the land, but they really don't. In less than 100 years, not a single person will own an inch of it—*someone else will own it all!*

People spend their entire lives attaining a certain level of wealth, and then they leave without it. It is such a waste. Consider the fact that many of us:

• grew up watching our parents pass like ships in the night, one leaving for work just as the other returned.

• watched one or both of our parents climb the financial Mt. Everest, forgetting who they were, what their priorities were, where they were going, and who they were married to.

• witnessed the person with the nicer clothes, bigger house, or faster car receive preferential treatment.

We learned through observation what was "right" and "normal," but we were never told there is more to the picture.

Stewardship

A steward is someone who manages what belongs to another person, and since God created the universe, everything is His. As objects of His creation, we are stewards, but never owners.

This stewardship reality affects us in every area, including finances, time, abilities, and children. God has merely entrusted it all to us for a time.

Why is stewardship so important? Because everyone who does not accept the position that we are stewards will fall far short of fulfilling God's will for their life. *We cannot honor God or fully achieve any goal when we believe we are owners.*

Why is stewardship so important to me? When I was in my 20s and doing well in the insurance business, my mother visited me and saw my home, my car, and other material possessions. She looked me in the eye and said, "Paul, I am frightened by your early success. Don't forget who gave you the talent, don't forget who owns it all, and don't let Satan use your success to take you away from what's important."

In 1969, she fell in her home and wasn't found for two days. (She died a few days later in the hospital with me holding her hand). In the apron she was wearing the day she fell, I found a note that read: "S.S. HOPE: 7 miles, 7 cents." I cried uncontrollably, realizing that she had raised 7 cents after walking 7 miles for S.S. HOPE, a hospital ship that provided medical care to people in developing nations. Her example was the most powerful act of stewardship I have ever witnessed!

Seven pillars of stewardship

There are seven foundational pillars that bring strength, wealth, and balance to individuals who recognize their role as steward.

Pillar #1 Pay God first with the tithe

I don't believe I am a good steward unless I tithe. Tithing (paying God 10 percent of the gross) is an integral part of stewardship because it accomplishes three primary objectives:

1) **It says who is Lord of your life.** (*"You cannot serve both God and Money"* Mathew 6:24.)

2) **It requires you to walk by faith.** (*"Without faith it is impossible to please God"* Hebrews 11:6.)

3) **It allows God to bless you.** (*"Then your barns will be filled to overflowing, and your vats will brim over with new wine"* Proverbs 3:10.)

I began tithing at age 27, thinking my 10 percent was pretty impressive, but at a speech by businessman and philanthropist Robert G. LeTourneau, I learned that he gave away 90 percent of his income and lived on the remaining 10 percent! So much for my arrogance on 10 percent!

I decided to give more—and the more I gave, the more God gave in return! My path of learning was not easy, however. Six months after I started tithing, I lost 90 percent of my net worth due to a business fiasco that I was not responsible for. Seeking answers, I read in Malachi 3:10, *"Bring all the tithes into the storehouse, that there may be food in my house."* It does not say to tithe *"when you can afford it"* or pay it with *"whatever is left over."* Tithing is a principle, whether you have a lot of money or not.

I tell people who ask for financial advice, "If you aren't tithing, then my counsel will do you no good. We are to pay our tithes first, then our taxes and bills." Perplexed, they often ask, "We are not paying our bills now, how are we supposed to tithe?"

The only time God ever challenges us to "try" Him in the entire Bible is in the area of tithing! He says in Malachi 3:10, *"Try me now in this ... if I will not open for you the windows of heaven and pour out for you such blessing that there will not have room enough to receive it."*

When I lost 90% of my income, I continued to tithe. Did God immediately pour out more blessings than I could contain? No, things actually went from bad to worse! But eventually, things changed for the better ... much better! God always keeps His promises.

Pillar #2 Keep commitments even when it hurts

When the tax laws on real estate changed in the early 1980s, I again found myself in financial difficulty. I had committed a certain amount each month to Christian organizations, but suddenly I was losing that same amount every month!

I sold properties and even took out loans to keep the commitments I had made. Bankers thought I was crazy, but I knew God would take care of me because His Word clearly states as much.

What happened? God blessed the work of my hands and I was able to keep every one of my commitments. Was it easy? No, but God provided for me, even when things looked impossible. (My financial books revealed that whenever a commitment was due, my income increased, and when a commitment was not due, my income dropped!)

Pillar #3 Be financially responsible.

Each of us is financially responsible for what we can control. God at least expects interest on what He gives us. The servant who buried his master's talent of gold instead of investing it was told, *"You ought to have deposited my money with the bankers, and at my coming I would have received back my own with interest"* (Matthew 25:27). God desires we multiply what He entrusts to us.

Do we make mistakes? Of course! I've lost money in investments and had numerous businesses close their doors. Am I a bad steward as a result? No! Winning over the long haul is what matters. Setbacks are never the end of the road.

> How much or how little we have is not nearly so important as what we do with it.

In addition to being responsible, we also need to be wise investors. I found a prime piece of real estate for sale, but a person with an "unsavory" business reputation owned it. Though I really wanted the property, I proceeded slowly and carefully. I had my attorney draft a comprehensive earnest-money deposit contract. The property owner signed the document, but kept stalling, hoping I would back out of the deal. After a couple of months, I asked if he was ready to close. He had no way of legally backing out of the contract—he knew it and his lawyer knew it. The property was mine in a few days!

Had I played by his rules, I would have lost my deposit and missed a great opportunity. Instead, I guarded my investment by doing due diligence. Scripture states, *"Be as wise as serpents and harmless as doves"* (Matthew 10:16). I sold the property several years later for five times what I paid for it!

Pillar #4 Give non-stop.

Givers will always give, regardless of how much or how little they have. Giving, at its core, is an attitude of the heart. When you give, everything about you will be tested.

Charlie "Tremendous" Jones said it perfectly, "You can't really enjoy anything without sharing it, and this includes your faith, love, talents and money. Someday you'll discover we never really give; we are only returning and sharing a small portion of what we've received."

And God will never allow you to give Him more than He gives back to you!

Pillar #5 Be faithful with what you have.

People who complain or wish they had what other people have are not good stewards over what God has entrusted to them. God gives seemingly small opportunities and we take it from there.

John Cook, a friend and business associate, was diagnosed with polio soon after his first child was born, and the doctors said he would be on an iron lung for the rest of his life. But John and his wife believed otherwise. He refused to give up, quit, or be defeated and was an inspiration to everyone he met. Soon he was off the machine and within two years, he was 90 percent restored! I was fortunate to hire him as my first employee. When he died in the fall of 2000, the world lost one of the best stewards of talents and abilities that I have ever known.

Pillar #6 Train others.

Stewards multiply themselves by training other people to be good stewards. This is especially effective with children. Howard Dayton, CEO of Crown Financial Ministries, says that children need training in four distinct areas: establishing routine responsibilities, exposure to work, earning extra money at home, and working for other people.

I taught my children early the concept of tithing, giving, saving, and investing. I am happy to say that all of them have made wise investments for their families here on earth and for their futures in heaven. They have taught their children the same principles of stewardship!

Pillar #7 Obey and trust toward God.

As a steward, it is my responsibility to do what God says to do. (The outcome is therefore His responsibility.) The rich young ruler in the Bible who went away sad when Jesus asked him to give away his wealth failed to understand that his obedience and trust toward God were all he had to offer. The wealth he "owned" was already God's!

When we give our obedience and trust to God, the doors of blessing open wide. God always does *"exceedingly abundantly above all that we ask or think"* (Ephesians 3:20).

When I was asked to speak at St. Andrews University in Scotland to the students, staff, and a large number of local pastors, I began by stating I wanted to take everyone's stewardship pulse. I asked them to take out their checkbooks and show me what they did with their money over the past 90 days. "It will tell me where your heart is," I explained.

I didn't actually look at their checkbooks, but it made them think. Churches would be radically different from what they are today if this principle was taught.

Our hearts are where our money is. It is our testimony.

The joy of giving

What makes being a good steward such a joy? Is it that you have something to be a steward with? That you are able to manage it wisely? That God has found you faithful with financial wealth?

Yes, but my greatest joy comes from giving it away. I once met a woman who was sacrificing her life, money, and time for the benefit of little children. I promised to help fund her dream. She was so thankful that she started to cry! Now past age 70, she is still going strong. I don't believe you can truly experience joy if you don't give your money away.

No joy matches my joy from giving. I've told wealthy businessmen, "You thought it was fun making it. Well, you don't know what fun is until you start giving it away."

> "The greater proportion of a man's income he gives, the happier he is."
>
> Patrick Morley

I tell my wife, Jane, "I feel guilty because I feel so hilariously happy today and explosive with joy." I may have less because I gave it away, but I gained much more in return.

We are simply stewards. Even the success we have is really His success—it's all His by right of creation.

My Work Is My Ministry

Freedom comes when they are one in the same.

To me, my work and ministry are one in the same. Scripture does not differentiate between work and ministry, secular and sacred. Instead, God says, *"Whatever you do in word or deed, do all in the name of the Lord Jesus"* (Colossians 3:17).

Noted speaker, Patrick Morley, author of the book *Man in the Mirror*, plainly states, "The issue isn't whether or not you are in ministry, but whether or not you are faithful in the ministry God has given you."

If we are not faithful in our work because we yearn to be "in the ministry," then we are doing a disservice to God, to ourselves, and others. In fact, I don't believe that until we are faithful where God places us will we ever be ready to fulfill our dreams.

Finding much-needed peace

You will find peace with God when you come to grips with the fact that doing what God has equipped and enabled you to do is most important, regardless of what or where that might be.

When I was 24 years old and excelling in the insurance business, I was invited to a meeting with 20 of North America's most influential preachers and speakers. In comparison to them, I felt like the only talent I had was making money. One of the men said, "Paul, God's will for your life might be to make money. Do what He has equipped and enabled you to do; *that* is your ministry."

> "95 percent of us will never be in 'occupational' ministry, but that does not mean we are not ministers."
>
> Patrick Morley

His comment brought great liberty to my heart and soul. I was freed from thinking I should be doing something more "meaningful." I could focus on what God had for me to do. (Making money was only a small part of that.)

Once and for all, we need to put to rest the notion that the only way to please God or to make an impact in the world is to be a minister of the gospel. Our work is not something we do until we have an opportunity to do ministry; it *is* ministry!

If you have been searching for your divine calling, you might find it right under your nose!

The exciting thrill of work

Most people are dissatisfied with their work, yet they stay in their current positions out of need, fear of change, lack of vision, or some other debilitating reason.

I was once asked to visit a 26-year-old man who was hospitalized with bleeding ulcers. After briefly getting acquainted, I looked him in the eye and asked, "If you had nobody to please in life, what would you do?" Through tears he sobbed, "I have always wanted to be a farmer."

Instead of pursuing his lifelong passion, he was in college working toward a degree he knew he didn't want to use! It was a nightmare for him, each day enduring a life he hated living.

I told him he needed to call in his family and tell them he could no longer live the life they were planning for him. He was trying too hard to be somebody he was not out of a misshapen sense of obedience and love for his parents and family. I watched him tell his family what had been on his heart for so many years, *and they finally understood!*

The doctor attending him, a friend of mine, told me that within 24 hours of the family confrontation, the young man's ulcers suddenly stopped bleeding! The young man walked out of the hospital, never to return again.

Today he is a farmer, owns a feed store, has a wife and kids, and is living the life he always wanted. He is one of the richest men I have ever known, not because of the money he makes, but because he is pursuing his life's dream.

Another time in a New York subway I sat beside a stockbroker, a man living the big life. In conversation, I mentioned the power and importance of goal setting and having right priorities. He actually bought one of my programs before reaching his station.

That night he wrote down everything he wanted to do in life and then said to his wife, "I just realized I'm not doing anything I really want to do."

With his wife's support, he quit his job and moved to Colorado. He put together a group of investors and went into the oil business. He drilled 13 dry holes, one after the other, but not one of the investors backed out. On the 14th hole, he hit the jackpot. Twenty more followed!

Though he is a multi-millionaire today, his satisfaction comes from doing what he loves to do. How wonderful to know my program made such a pivotal move with his family possible.

How many people are in careers or colleges who don't belong there? Will each of us be able to say to God, "I used the talents and abilities that you gave me to their fullest potential"?

Be the example.

How we work is the best example of who we really are on the inside. Add the money ingredient, however, and people's ethics often become "situational ethics."

My friend Bill Nix knows this too well. As an investment banker, he was once poised to make two million dollars on a 500 million-dollar construction project. Everything was on target until a representative from the bank called and asked for $10,000 in cash to "make sure everything worked smoothly." Bill knew it was a bribe and said he wouldn't do it. The phone went dead and the deal stopped cold.

For Bill, two million dollars wasn't enough to waiver on his ethics. No price was high enough because he had decided long ago he would remain true to God's Word, regardless of the situation.

History reveals that Sir Arthur Conan Doyle once played a practical joke on twelve respected and well-known men whom he knew. He sent out twelve telegrams all with the same message: "Flee at once. All is discovered." Within 24 hours, they had all left the country! Each of these men obviously had something to hide.

That is not the way you want to live!

Combine faith with works.

Mankind has always tried to gain right standing with God by doing good works. This work-your-way-to-heaven approach is the basis for many religions, but not with Christianity. (If it were, there would have been no need for Jesus to die on the cross.)

> Good works without faith aren't worth anything, at least from God's perspective.

We gain nothing through good works because *"By grace you have been saved through faith ... not of works"* (Ephesians 2:8-9). Good works by themselves lead to legalism and bondage, while faith alone is little more than hot air. Combine the two and God's will is accomplished and people's lives are changed.

Recently I read about a boy who needed a very expensive surgery. His parents could not afford the operation, much less the flight to Houston. I spoke with several doctors who agreed to operate at no charge and then I chartered a plane and flew the boy to Houston where he had the 5-hour surgery.

His mother said, "I have heard of people helping others, but I've never seen it with my own eyes." How sad!

Another time I met a man who was facing increased health problems and a business that he could not handle. With only a meager retirement, he was in trouble. I showed him how to use his business to fund his retirement. This advice was the answer to his dilemma and he is now financially set for the rest of his life.

We were all created to accomplish great things!

The bottom line when work is ministry

At times I've been invited to speak and before I went on stage the coordinator would say, "Don't mention Jesus or God, OK? We don't want to offend anyone."

I always smile and thank them, and then tell the audience I always want to know from what basis a speaker is supporting their beliefs, principles, and advice. I tell them that my beliefs are based on God and His Word. As a listener, I would expect nothing less.

It is important that everyone have the same chance I did to reach their full potential. I believe that without Jesus Christ, it is impossible that they ever will. This view has sparked countless debates, letters to the editor in local newspapers, phone calls, discussions, rebukes, and more. *Newsweek* magazine called me a "jug-eared evangelist" because of my big ears and because of what I said. It doesn't matter to me. My hope is that someone will come to the freeing, saving and incredible knowledge of Jesus Christ through what I do and what I say.

That is the bottom line reason *my work is my ministry*.

The True Role
of an Employer

Business is better when employers know their role.

Have you ever felt "expendable" as an employee? I can relate. One company hired me to help them through a tight financial spot, firing me when their revenue increased.

Intuitively, employers know they would be nowhere without their employees and that sending an employee away angry might hurt business in the long run, yet every day another "expendable" employee is fired.

Why is that? I believe the reason is that employers don't understand their true role is actually that of a servant.

Serving is good business.

Employees work harder when I serve them, which makes me want to serve them even more. Then they are more committed and willing to grow, and I want to help them in return—and the cycle continues.

Perpetual motion in business is about serving and the benefits that result. As a servant leader, I purpose to:

#1) Provide—much more than money

Businesses exist to make money, but with the many components (products, services, overhead, salaries, etc.) there is one part that is often overlooked: the employees.

As an employer, if I can help my employees reach their goals, they will help me toward mine—in that order.

In the mid 1970s I asked Joe Baxter, a capable and trustworthy manager within my company, what he would do if he could do anything he wanted to. Without hesitation he said, "I would travel the world."

At that time I needed someone to manage our growing international business, so that very day I made him a proposal that included two conditions I was sure he would like:

• You can't travel to any country without your wife. (The better his marriage, the better his long-term performance.)

• You have to take time off while overseas. (If he relaxes and enjoys what he does, he will perform better on the job.)

He jumped at the opportunity and has since traveled to 101 different countries and set up businesses in over 60 of them! Now retired, Joe recently told me, "I lived a life that only few men ever dream of, thanks to you."

Actually, the opportunity I gave Joe was really for my benefit. I saw it as an investment. The ideas he generated and businesses he established have brought in tens of millions of dollars!

The late Cecil Day, one of the most respected businessmen of all time and the founder of Days Inns, once paid a farmer twice the asking price for the property. "A deal is only a deal when it's a good deal for both parties," he said.

Employees should be served, not just because it is good business, but also because it is the right thing to do.

#2) Protect—for them and for you.

Several years ago one of my employees flew to Florida for eye surgery. I realized she would have to fly back on the same airline, being exposed to germs, crowds, disruptive schedules, cramped conditions, etc. I called her and said, "I'm sending my Leer jet to pick you up. You'll be home in half the time."

She was so happy and relieved that she burst into tears, but in protecting her, I was doing myself a favor. She does a better job than

I ever could, which means the better I treat her and protect her, the more my companies prosper.

Regarding the belief that "burnout is inevitable," I believe if the employer is paying careful attention to the needs of the employees, burnout is avoidable. By treating my employees as I would like to be treated, we all win.

#3) Give respect—they deserve it.

Without employees, we are forever limited to what we can do by ourselves. When you add in capable and creative people, you have the potential for unlimited, exponential increase in productivity. We must let them know that we appreciate, need, and respect them. Giving employees the respect they deserve will enable them to be more confident, creative, understanding, giving, and profitable.

The employer and employee must have a system in place that provides for necessary communication. Companies can grow to the point that a manager cannot talk face to face with every employee, which is fine, but respect for employees must always remain a part of an employer's temperament.

A wise businessman once told me, "I tell every new employee, 'You do not work *for* me, but *with* me.'"

#4) Be trustworthy—a must.

We all know bosses and managers who promise a raise or promotion, but never follow through. Crushing an employee's hopes completely undermines trust and long-term success.

If we are trustworthy, our employees will trust us, but to the extent that there is selfishness, stinginess, or lying in us, they will know it! And over time, that will erode trust.

Being trustworthy involves listening to our employees. I heard of a man who had a great cost-reducing proposal. When he submitted his idea to his supervisor, he was curtly told, "We don't pay you to think; we pay you to work." Years later the idea was finally implemented, resulting in the company saving $500,000 the first year!

Another trust-builder is to help meet employee's personal needs. If something happens like a death in the family or a divorce, the employee's work is affected. To neglect these very real problems can hurt both you and your employees.

Several years ago I started using chaplains from Marketplace Ministries to help my employees with their personal concerns (as part of their benefit package). These chaplains show up on a regular basis and are available to talk, pray, counsel, and listen confidentially.

Marketplace Ministries, founded by Gil A. Stricklin in 1984, is in more than 225 cities in 32 states with over 900 chaplains and is designed to take care of a company's most important asset: employees and their families. Increased loyalty to the company, reduction in absenteeism, increased productivity, and reduction in employee turnover are just a few of the dividends gained by partnering with Marketplace Ministries.

Whatever is required to be trustworthy, it is worth it … and it will show on the bottom line.

#5) Give direction—leading the way.

Employers must take an active role in assisting their employees to meet their goals. Occasionally, you may lose a talented employee to another company, but if you were the employee, wouldn't you appreciate a hand toward reaching your goals?

I had a very bright woman working in one of our companies making approximately $25,000 a year. I realized she had talent over and above what was needed in her position so I introduced her to a friend of mine in another company. Within 90 days she had a new job, making 75 percent more than we were paying her!

Sometimes providing direction means discipline and correction. I called a manager, who was having serious financial problems, into mt office. I told him up front, "I'm not going to fire you; I want to help you solve your problems." I had him sit down with an accountant who helped him find a workable solution to what seemed to be ruining his life. He benefited, and so did I.

Walt Wiley of the Fellowship of Companies for Christ International wisely states, "A servant leader leads for the primary benefit of those who follow."

#6) Provide training—preparing for success.

I take advice and training seriously. Through it my employees get better, the company gets better, and the clients and customers are better served. Some might move on to bigger and better things, like my son Larry after 10 years, but it is to their benefit.

Not long ago I helped a young lady in one of our companies by paying for night classes. She graduated with her degree and now has a better job. Giving her the time, money, and opportunity was to my benefit because a learning company is also a growing company.

> If it's the employer's fault that his employees aren't trained, then firing everyone is not the answer.

In fact, more than 50 profitable businesses in my hometown have come from individuals who once worked for me. Trying to "force" them to stay with me would have done more harm than good.

Some employers don't train their employees and then complain that they aren't worth their wages and deserve to be fired, but having untrained employees is the fault of the employer. Well-trained employees are always one of an employer's greatest assets.

#7) Place people over product—at all costs.

Most employers are more focused on what they do than on the people who work for them. This is a very easy trap to fall into, since without the product or service, the job wouldn't even exist.

Granted, both the product and the person are obviously necessary, but employees who feel they are less important than the work they perform will be dissatisfied and will not be the stellar employees that they could be.

My focus is first on my employees, then on what they do. This does not lessen the importance of quality work, but has a unique way of making the product even better.

Sometimes, placing people over a product will cost you personally. I've paid tens of thousands of dollars for employees to stay home and deal with family issues, take education classes, fly to another city for

> "Any definition of success must include service in it somewhere."
> Former President
> George H.W. Bush

a needed vacation, and more. In addition to money, I've also spent considerable time with employees and their families, counseling, giving advice, training, or even helping them arrange financing for a home.

Placing people over product is just the right thing to do.

Application in business

It is not a legal requirement for employers to apply these principles, but I do believe it is a moral requirement for Christian employers.

I have done my best to apply these principles myself, and though I have made mistakes, I am very fortunate to work with the most loyal group of people on earth. There isn't anything they wouldn't do for me, and there isn't anything I wouldn't do for them.

This mutual service comes from a genuine love for God. From that, I have a strong desire to serve others, to help them, and to bless them, all because God has done this, and so much more, for me!

Jesus said, *"If anyone desires to be first, he shall be last of all and the servant of all"* (Mark 9:35). After training, teaching, encouraging, and correcting His disciples, Jesus washed their feet—a massive statement of humility—then He went even further and died on the cross for them!

I can't top His act of service, but it stands as a stark reminder to me of how much service I can give.

The Greatest Success of All
Knowing God

As a boy, my family was never financially well off. However, during World War II, we sent some of what we did have to relatives in war-torn Europe. Every few weeks I helped my dad box up and send small cartons of dried fruit, jams, nuts, etc. Perhaps the food ended up on the table of an enemy soldier or in the hands of a hungry mailman. We never knew, but my dad thought it was important, so I helped him.

Over 50 years later, after tracking down some of my parent's ancestors in France and Germany, I found myself at the home of the very family we had mailed the packages to years before. As we chatted, the discussion turned to World War II and I asked my cousin if they ever received the boxes my father and I had sent.

His eyes brimmed with tears and his voice cracked as he explained, "We survived because of what you mailed to us. We would not have made it otherwise."

All the work and effort were instantly worth it as he gave me a hug filled with such gratitude that I too began to weep.

My level of trust for my dad went up several notches that day. If he were still alive and wanted me to send a care package to someone, I wouldn't hesitate. Why? I knew him well enough to trust him completely.

Trusting comes from knowing.

In the same way, the more we know God, the more we will trust Him. J. I. Packer, author of *Knowing God*, says that God takes people (i.e., Jacob, Joseph, and others) to the bottom of life so that they can ultimately live at the top. Why does God do this? Because getting us where he wants us to go always involves trusting Him.

Whether going to the absolute bottom is mandatory or not, I cannot say. I know, however, that I've been to the bottom several times and it was worth it every time! What I gained in the knowledge and trust of God I would not trade for the world.

It wasn't a piece of cake, but it sure was good for me. The bottom line is that God wants me to trust Him, and though He will never force me, He will go to great lengths for that to happen—and He does this for everyone!

Experiencing God authors, Henry T. Blackaby and Claude V. King, explain that God uses us for something "big" when we are truly ready … and we become ready by knowing and trusting God.

> "God wants us to know Him deeply because He knows what knowing Him will do for us."
>
> Peter V. Deison

Abraham, one of my favorite men in the Bible, made plenty of mistakes, but he never quit. He desired to obey God with all his heart. When God told him to sacrifice his only son Isaac, he obeyed. At the last second, an angel showed him a ram that he sacrificed instead. Through his obedience he discovered more of God's character and saw how God was able to provide for him.

I have seen God provide many times and my faith and trust toward God have grown each time. As Abraham, I don't always see the end result of my actions, but I still obey in faith. For instance, I've felt I should help certain people financially, only to discover they were taking advantage of me. Didn't God know that? Of course He did, but my job is to be obedient, not to know all the answers. Through my obedience, I know God better, which is probably the whole point.

When all was said and done, Abraham knew God on a personal level. He understood His character and found Him to be trustworthy. In fact, Abraham went on to be called a friend of God's. Now that is a success!

Where trust will lead you
Trusting God will require two choices that nobody else can make for you. The first decision is the most important one:

1) Do you trust God with your eternity?
When I was 16 years old and standing alone in a grape vineyard, I made that decision. Jesus said, *"I am the door: If anyone enters by Me, he will be saved"* (John 10:9). Though my mother led me to that door, I made the willful choice to confess my sins and ask Jesus into my heart.

The more I learned of God's character and His love for me, the more I trusted Him.

> "I thank God today for the hard, harsh, abrasive times that raked my emotions and absolutely pulled out from under me the thing that I was hanging on to ... so that there was nothing left but God."
>
> Chuch Swindoll

2) Do you trust God with your daily life?
Eternity is forever, while a mere 70 to 90 years on earth is nothing more than a drop in an ocean-size bucket. Why are we quick to trust God with our eternity, yet we struggle with trusting Him in our daily lives?

What would cause a person not to trust God? After all, He is never late, never unfaithful, never cruel, never absent, never unloving, and never wrong. Have we been preconditioned to believe otherwise?

If you, as I, have had plenty of trust-defeating experiences, don't hold that against God. We can trust God because He is *"a God of truth and without injustice; righteous and upright is He"* (Deuteronomy 32:4) who desires that we experience *"life, and that they may have it more abundantly"* (John 10:10).

121

God is trustworthy, perfect, and on your side. How can you not love Him?

Loving God

God doesn't offer only select people the opportunity to know Him. Instead, He wants to have a personal relationship with everyone, but He will never impose.

Is it possible to know God as you know your best friend? Yes, though you obviously cannot sit down with God and have a cup of coffee together. The relationship is different, yet it's the same—even better!

Going for a walk with my wife is the method by which I get to know her. What we do is not as important as the fact that I am listening and seeking to understand her.

Christians have sought to know God for generations, yet ask questions like: "How many chapters do I need to read in the Bible? How long should I pray? What happens if I miss one day? Is 10 minutes long enough?"

Such questions miss the point. They focus on the *method* instead of the *reason*, which is legalistic and will stifle any relationship. I spend time with my wife because I love her, not because I am ordered to. In relation to God, our love for Him is not limited to something like an emotional high from a certain experience. We are to love Him with everything we are, wholly and completely.

The more you love, the more you know Him—and the more you know Him, the more you love.

Obeying God

Obedience is the next part of a relationship with God, but before you can obey, you must know what He is telling you to do.

God seldom speaks audibly, though He does speak constantly through His Word and His Holy Spirit. (He also speaks through other people, circumstances, and more—and everything He says is in line with His character and His Word.)

When I made Him Lord of my life, I gave up the right to say "no" to His commands. When He speaks, I obey. That is where growth, breakthrough, and blessing take place.

Years ago I had an especially pivotal breakthrough in my knowledge of God. I had invested a lot of time, energy, and money into a business venture that was ready to be launched. However, I suddenly found myself in a difficult situation: proceed against my morals and business ethics based on God's Word or let the business die at the starting gate. I chose the second option.

> "What a man truly knows, he will love, and what he truly loves, he will serve."
> Dr. Dwight Pentecost

Within days I was offered an opportunity that eventually led me to where I am today. Through that experience I came to understand that God was even more interested in my welfare than I was! By obeying Him, I benefited in every way.

Serving God

Serving God is the last part of knowing Him. People who place serving first often accomplish great things for God, but many fail to have a personal relationship with Him along the way.

Scripture plainly states, *And this is eternal life, that they may know You, the only true God, and Jesus Christ whom You have sent* (John 17:3). Since knowing God is eternal life, it makes sense that we should focus on knowing God rather than on serving Him.

This by no means minimizes the importance of serving. We usually end up serving Him as a result of obedience. Some of the most meaningful and enjoyable times in life have come as I obeyed God by serving others.

• I've given my coat to someone who needed it more than I did. I was so warmed on the inside, I could have stayed outside in the cold all day!

• I've helped hundreds of young people go to college. I am incredibly excited about their futures and love playing a part in them!

- I've helped take care of my employees in many ways. I always end up being more blessed in return!
- I've given to organizations that help the homeless, the rejected, and the hungry. I am humbled yet invigorated as I help!

Happiness that comes through service that originated in obedience is so intense that words can't describe it! You will have to experience it for yourself!

Knowing God's heart

Peter V. Deison, author of *The Priority of Knowing God*, wrote, "God wants us to know Him deeply because He knows what knowing Him will do for us."

> "It is easy to know a lot about God while not knowing much of God. We can even be good without knowing God."
>
> J. I. Packer

That is precisely God's heart. He gives back far more than we could ever give to Him. He loves to bless us, give to us, and be with us simply because He is our Father.

Knowing God is the greatest success of all!

Walking with Christ

The life-long journey that never ends

Is it hard to follow God? It depends on your definition of "hard." Does following God come with a cost? Absolutely! Are there wants and desires that you give up? All the time! But is it hard to follow Him? The answer is a resounding, "No!"

Cost and self-sacrifice do not make something hard. Nobody feels sorry for the athlete who wins an Olympic medal, even though it required grueling effort behind the scenes, all for one brief moment of glory. The medal, once attained, minimizes every cost.

While there are costs and self-sacrifices to be made, that does not mean it is hard to follow God. "Hard" is when you compete but never win, invest but lose everything, work but receive nothing for your efforts, and show love but receive hate in return. *That* would be a hard life, but that is not the life I have lived!

What does it mean to follow God?
In every paradigm (sheep and Shepherd, servant and Master, creation and Creator, etc.), I am the follower and He is the leader. But God is so much more! Scripture says He is:

- my father (Romans 8:15)
- my brother (Hebrews 2:11)
- my intercessor (Romans 8:34)
- the atoning sacrifice for my sins (I John 2:2)

In addition, Scriptures says that I am:
- a child of God (Romans 8:16)
- a new creation (II Corinthians 5:17)
- a joint-heir with Christ (Romans 8:17)

When I learned that Christ was my Lord and Savior AND my brother, intercessor, father, and even friend, my perception of Christ and my relationship to Him changed dramatically! Now we could actually walk together!

Jesus initially greeted His future disciples with, "Come, follow me," but He didn't tell them the same thing every day because they were already *with* Him. Scripture says that Jesus lives *in* us (I John 3:24) and because He is already in me, I don't need to chase after Him. We are inseparably linked. Jesus adds, *"I will never leave you nor forsake you"* (Hebrews 13:5).

Clearly, God wants more of a relationship with me than a slave has with his master or a king with his subjects. I find it amazing that God would allow me, a man who grew up as a fruit picker in California who at times had a foul mouth and who never earned a college degree, to inherit everything that He has for me! Why would God do that?

There is one word to describe it: *grace*.

The journey of grace

People often use the word grace, but seldom understand its meaning. Grace is not to be confused with mercy. Mercy is letting you off the hook for something you did or rightly deserve. Grace is giving you something you do not deserve and could not gain, buy, or earn, no matter how hard you try.

> "Grace means that God does it all."
>
> Steve McVey

We do not deserve all that God has given us, no matter how morally upright we might try to be. We have all sinned and death should be our lot in life as sinners, but God has given us life that overflows with His goodness, kindness, and generosity. God does nothing half way! He said, *"I have come that they may have life, and that they may have it more abundantly"* (John 10:10).

He gives me what I don't deserve, He desires to bless me beyond what I can handle, and then He dies for me! What type of one-sided relationship is that?

As you journey with Christ, there are countless detours that falsely promise a better way, an easier way, or a smoother way. I have encountered three detours along the way. They are reccurring and sneaky. Thankfully, God provided the Holy Spirit to help us get back on track through repentance and forgiveness. Here are the three detours:

Detour #1   The Path of Least Resistance

If I choose not to obey God and instead do what I want to do, I have just taken the path of least resistance. This detour becomes viable when I begin to think, "I'm tired of giving up my wants and dreams. What I want is more important."

God does not ask us to give up everything, but there are times when His plans and our plans do not match. When we die to our own agenda and obey what He says to do, we stay on course. When I disobey and do what I want, it ends up hurting me more in the long run than if I had obeyed God in the first place.

> "The course of least resistance makes crooked rivers and crooked men."
> William Danforth

This dying to self does not guarantee smooth sailing, but obstacles along God's path are designed to mature me, while obstacles on the detour are there to destroy me.

In my youth, I did not understand that dying to self is the first part of the overall process of preparation; the second part is God rebuilding me. Isaiah 64:8 says, *"We are the clay, and You our potter."* Through repetitive rebuilding I become pure, clean, and whole, which is only possible when He removes my selfishness from the equation.

Taking the path of least resistance is not always a defiant act of rebellion. I may want to accomplish God's will, but if I try and do it in my own strength, I am taking the path of least resistance and am on a detour nonetheless.

The more I understand the process of preparation, the more I allow my selfish ambitions to die. As a result, I have willingly traded:

- my wants for His wants
- my "big" dreams for His dreams
- my plans for His plans
- my goals for His goals
- my abilities for His abilities
- my gifts for His gifts
- my hopes for His hopes
- my life for His life

In each of these cases, I've come out better off than before! God is a giver and not a taker; He always reciprocates to a larger degree. The path of least resistance, however, is nothing more than a dead-end road.

Detour #2 Saved by Grace, Living by Works

Scripture states, *"By grace you have been saved"* (Ephesians 2:8). Nobody deserves salvation and there is not a single person who could work his or her way to heaven. Nonetheless, good works have been mankind's "best shot" at salvation for thousands of years.

> Denying self treats the symptoms; dying to self solves the problem.

After people find salvation by grace in Jesus Christ, they often start relying on good works as a basis for maintaining their right standing with God. I know I have been down this detour many times myself before I repented and got back on track.

The truth is, I cannot live the perfect Christian life. I'll never be good enough or do enough good deeds to please God. It is not possible! Reliance on good works is a detour that separates me from my relationship with Christ.

God is perfect and He demands perfection, but when I surrender my life to Jesus, God accepts me. My righteousness is not from what I do, but from who I am as a believer in Christ. Because of this grace:

- God expects nothing in return for what He has done for me.
- God will never give up on me.
- God sees me as righteous.
- God doesn't want me to lead others to morality, but to Christ.

Is it possible to take grace too far, doing my own thing, living a life that is an embarrassment to Christ? Not if I love God, because if I love God, I will do what pleases Him. In essence, I am free to do whatever I want since what I want is what God wants.

Am I weak because I recognize that I cannot do things in my own strength? No, I am strong, because, as God Himself says, *"My grace is sufficient for you, for My strength is made perfect in weakness"* (2 Corinthians 12:9).

Accepting the fact that God uses my weaknesses has been difficult for me. I had a German father who told me on more than one occasion, "God gave you a brain; use it!" The subconscious message was to become self-sufficient.

My mother said, "You have everything you need to succeed right between your ears." The message was that I was the fertile ground and just needed to plant the right seeds. Again, the implication was that I needed only to exercise my initiative to make things happen.

Today I recognize that it is simply impossible for me to live the Christian life in my own strength. I need to trust Jesus Christ to be Himself in and through me. Because of His grace, that is enough!

Detour #3 Wanting to Be Like Christ

My greatest desire as I journeyed with Christ was to be like Him. I wanted to love like He loved, give like He gave, and serve like He served. I desired to imitate Him in every area.

Though this is a noble goal and sounds "Christian," it is not biblical. God does not want me to be like Christ for several reasons:

1. It is impossible for me to be perfect like Christ.
2. It excludes Him from working in my life.
3. It leads me toward good works as a means of salvation, which is unbiblical and religious.
4. It sets me up for a fall.

Not only is trying to imitate Christ an effort in futility, it is also wrong. I knew that salvation required that I accept Christ by faith, but trying to be like Christ seemed an appropriate goal as a Christian. I didn't realize that Christ placed His life into me so that He could live His life through me. My walk with Christ has nothing to do with me imitating Him and everything to do with me walking, living, and breathing with Him.

I can't do what He did! Nobody can. Where does that leave me? It leaves me in a better position than I could have imagined! My heart, mind, and soul are freed from the shackles of performance and religion.

Here is the amazing truth: as I walk with Christ and allow Him to work in and through me, I end up acting like Him anyway! I don't need to try to be like Him—I am like Him because He is in me.

Finding God's Will
for Your Life

Answering the question that everyone has asked

Finding God's will for my life was not easy. Not that God was keeping it a secret or that I wasn't willing to follow Him, but rather that I just didn't know how to blend His will into my life and make it work.

"Full speed ahead" has always been my approach. I jump in with everything I have to accomplish a goal. Add in my mother's Scottish determination and nothing could stand in my way!

I found with my inner drive and natural gifts it was easy to leave God out of the picture. I can set any goal and achieve it, but that may or may not be God's will.

Before I could focus on accomplishing God's will, I first needed to learn how to handle myself.

His will, my will, and me

Being goal oriented, doggedly determined, and highly motivated makes for an interesting combination. It has its benefits and its drawbacks, but so it is with every person. Some have intellectual conflicts, power conflicts, authority conflicts, or insecurity conflicts. Additionally, Christians struggle between their wants and the wants of the Holy Spirit.

Mentally and emotionally I could turn my will over to God, but reality was another matter. About half of the time I was seeking God's will, the other half mine.

> Asking God what to do in every little detail is not faith at all. It is immaturity.

When a great business idea would go up in smoke, I would at least accept responsibility for my actions, but I would kick myself for not asking God for His will first.

A good friend once confided, "I have struggled with finding God's will for my life because I wanted Him to help me with my will rather than me helping Him with His will."

The more we see ourselves for who we are (limited in every respect) and the more we see Him for who He is (unlimited in every respect), the less we will demand our own way.

The answers began to fall into place when I started to daily apply Scripture to my prayer life, my thought life, and my physical life. Matthew 6:33 states, *"Seek first the kingdom of God and His righteousness, and all these things shall be added to you."*

I also prayed every day for wisdom, then proceeded like He answered my prayer.

God's will for your life

There are more books, cassettes and seminars on finding the will of God than ever in the history of man, yet the same question continues to surface.

Why is that? The reason is that there are seven interrelated parts (like pieces in a puzzle) in our pursuit of God's will that must be assembled and most people haven't put all seven pieces together. And if you leave one out, your puzzle is incomplete.

#1 Big plans

You must believe that God does have a plan for your life because you are in His family. He created you, adopted you into His family, and made you a son or daughter (Ephesians 1:5). And as an heir, He has big plans for you!

#2 His will

To sincerely desire to do His will means including God in every aspect of your goal-setting process. This requires a heart attitude of, "Not my will but Yours be done." Then listen, watch, wait patiently, and let Him show you His will as you go about your daily routine.

#3 His Word

You need to continuously search His Word (the Bible) for direction. Then you will continually be pointed in the right direction (toward Christ). As you do this, God will equip you to know and live His perfect plan for your life.

#4 Accept responsibility

I've heard all types of prayers, from, "God, what color should I paint my bedroom?" to "Should I take my umbrella with me today?" I personally don't think God cares the slightest about the color of our room or whether we carry an umbrella.

Asking God what to do in every little detail is not faith at all. It is immaturity, evidence that a person would rather be told what to do than to take responsibility for his or her own actions. By faith, we must believe we are walking in God's wisdom and maintain balance through the use of common sense.

#5 Give up control

Giving up control does not mean you submit to other people, doing exactly what they say, nor do you wait around for God to tell you what to do. Rather, it means that you are "leadable," which entails being:

1. in motion (moving toward your goals)
2. willing to do what God says (humble and teachable)

Trust that God will communicate with you through His Holy Spirit. And if you mess up, God is big enough to fix anything you might break along the way. Don't put pressure on yourself to be perfect. If you make a mistake, learn from it, then move forward toward Him, knowing *"All things work together for good to those who love God, to those who are the called according to His purpose"* (Romans 8:28).

#6 Even in hard times

Walking in the will of God is intended to be a lifelong journey. He never takes vacations, siestas, or the weekend off. He is always watching over you and directing your steps, even during the hard times.

Sometimes God interrupts what we want because He knows it would be wrong for us. Years ago I wanted to go into a certain business and did everything I could think of to make it a reality. I confess I didn't ask God first; I simply proceeded, but God kept slamming the door shut!

As I spent time in Scripture and in prayer, God revealed what His perfect plans were. My plans turned out to be miniscule in comparison to His, and the door He opened no one could close, just like His Word says, *"I have set before you an open door, and no one can shut it"* (Revelation 3:8). His plans were beyond my imagination!

#7 Trust Him

The last piece of the puzzle is often the most difficult to apply. In summary it asks: do we really trust God?

"In His will is our peace."

Dante

I've been through things, both very good and very bad, that could have hurt me (my wife, family, business, etc.) tremendously had I not trusted and obeyed God. He has told me to do things that didn't make sense by applying conventional wisdom, but I have learned to trust Him despite what others or I might say or think. He has been proven trustworthy every time!

I believe God will not only take care of you, but His will for your life is far greater than you could ever ask or imagine!

Is there a guarantee?

How do you guarantee you will walk in God's will? By making Him Lord of your life and placing your will under His. From there, He can direct the desires He gives you or has already given you.

By giving us dreams and visions for our future, He takes a chance we won't run ahead and attempt to accomplish them ourselves. If we truly want to do His will (and realize we can't do it on our own), then we need to do it His way.

I finally got it through my aggressive head that if I wanted to accomplish His will, I needed to slow down, be patient, and walk in His wisdom. As I did, I found myself right where I needed to be.

Why isn't the will of God instant, easy, and painless?

Finding the will of God is obviously important, but our tendency is to always think in terms of what we do for God. After all, accomplishing His will is our goal.

It would be easy if God gave each of us an outline of our future with specific directions. But if He wanted robots, He would have created robots. Instead, He equips us with free will because there can be no relationship where free will is absent. His will for your life is only part of the whole picture. He wants a relationship.

When we choose to submit our will to His, He loves it. When He blesses us with peace and fulfillment, we love it (and so does He).

The bottom line is that God is really more concerned with your heart than He is with what you might do for Him. That is why finding and accomplishing His will is a lifelong pursuit. He is working on you (who you are) at the same time He is working through you (what you do for Him).

The end result will surpass your greatest expectations!

How I Want to Be Remembered

What the bottom line really looks like up close

There is old saying that if you want to know how people will talk about you when you are gone, write your own epitaph now and then live that way!

What would your epitaph say? How do you want to be remembered?

Epitaphs are usually one-liners that capture the essence of a person's life. Since there is no rule that prohibits having more than one epitaph, here are 13 epitaphs I would choose for myself:

1.   He loved God first.
2.   He loved his family and extended family.
3.   He loved his friends.
4.   He was a giver.
5.   He was an encourager.
6.   He forgave!.
7.   He kept his word.
8.   He honored God with his life.
9.   He always had a POSITIVE attitude.
10. He was not ashamed of the gospel of Jesus Christ.
11. He was a role model.
12. He contributed to his community.
13. He consistently helped others.

> We will be remembered for what we actually do, not what we wish we had done.

What others say about you

Although we like great things said about us, it all comes down to the reality of our actions. What we do has a greater impact than anything we say.

Over the years I have kept thank-you notes, letters, and cards that people have sent me. Their comments encourage me greatly, and though many claim to have been blessed by me, I can honestly say I was more blessed by giving than they were by receiving.

Here is a sampling of the kind notes I have received:

"Thank you so very much for the $500.00 donation when our house burned. That was truly the nicest thing anybody ever did for us."
– Sandy

"Thank you for all the material on cancer. I've been trying to read as much as possible on diets as well as alternative treatments. Today I started the 3rd chemo treatment in a series of 6. One must try to keep a positive attitude. Sunday I started to read again the book you sent. Please keep us in your prayers." – Millie

"I want to begin by saying how much I appreciate your generous donation to my recent mission trip to Algiers, Spain. It enabled me to have a life-changing experience that I will not forget."
– Jared

> "The Golden Rule is of no use to you whatsoever unless you realize that it is your move."
>
> Dr. Frank Crane

"I don't know how to thank you for what you have done [paying for her son to attend Bible college]. I don't know how to thank God either, but I know you are working together on this. How can I thank you for doing something so huge. I will be grateful always. Every time I think about it I cry ... Thank you from the bottom of my heart." – Inez

I am honored to have played just a small part in helping make their lives a little better. Helping always does me more good than it does them. (In fact, I should be the one writing the letters!)

How will we be remembered in 100 years?

Not one of us will be here in 100 years, but the question for me is, "What will people be saying about me a 100 years from now?"

A long-time friend, Harold Keown, Sr., will probably not be remembered for having the world's largest collection of personal-development books, though that is true, but for his kind treatment of other people.

Though I know Harold through hours of talking, I have never known my great-grandparents hopes and dreams, what they believed in or what they wanted to accomplish. Much has been lost in each of our families, which is why we owe it to those who come after us to put those answers in a book, a video, or another format they can use.

One more chance

When I was 12 years old and in the Boy Scouts, my best friend, Billy Farnham, and I went camping with 3,000 other Scouts in the mountains of California. During the night Billy lit a candle inside our tent (perhaps he was scared) and then fell asleep. The candle ignited his sleeping bag and he burned to death. I escaped without a scratch. I promised Billy's father, who was the scoutmaster, that I would grow up to be a Scout for both of us. But I still wondered, "Why him and not me?"

> "Reason, too late perhaps, may convince you of the folly of misspending time."
>
> George Washington

We don't always get a second chance. As adults, we often miss what is most important in life until it is too late. Many people could easily interchange their name for Joe's in the following story:

On his deathbed, Joe's family asked him what he wished he had done while he still could. Instead of listing all the things he had spent years pursuing and dreaming about, such as a bigger house, the ultimate job, more investments, better vacations, etc., Joe's wish list was short and simple.

He wished he had spent more time with his family, gone to Europe with Marge, his wife, attended his kid's ballgames, taken his grandkids out for lunch more often, and not worked as much. The only reference to work was wishing he had done less of it.

> Do today what you will wish you had done tomorrow.

During life's most trying times, what is most important instantly comes to the surface while the unimportant suddenly becomes inconsequential. Sadly, many come to that revelation too late.

A long time ago I purposed that I would do today what I would wish I had done tomorrow. This perspective allows me to enjoy many special times with other people. Recently, I took the day off from work to spend time with three of my granddaughters, 4-wheeling on my ranch and skipping stones in a creek. I don't know who had more fun, them or me.

I know a young dad who went through his parent's 8-mm film collection, having it converted into VHS format. He told me, "The entire collection of film was a mere 20 minutes long!" The potential had been there to capture more of his life history, but the opportunity was gone.

We cannot afford to lose a single moment. Life is just too short! I want to make the most of every day because tomorrow is not guaranteed. One of my favorite sayings is "carpe diem," which means, "seize the day."

Habits that help you "seize the day"

I believe there are certain habits that will enable us to live life to its fullest, making the most of every opportunity. These habits are not personality traits! They are little choices that we internalize into habits.

Here are 13 of my favorite habits that help me seize each day:

1. Be an inverted paranoid: I believe the whole world is conspiring to do only good things to me.

2. Be a quick forgiver: I don't have time to waste in unforgiveness.

3. Be optimistic: Believing the best of people and circumstances is a sure way to find the best.

4. Be thankful: I always give thanks, keep my eyes on God as my provider, and keep a smile on my face.

5. Be an encourager: Encouragers make me feel better, stronger, and more capable of accomplishing my dreams. I want to do the same for others.

6. Be spontaneous: I have a sense of urgency and a do-it-now attitude.

7. Be a giver: My greatest joy is giving!

8. Be positive: Being positive has the potential of turning the worst situations into victories.

9. Smile a lot and laugh at life: Adversity is a stepping-stone, not a roadblock. Why not laugh in the midst of the challenges?

10. Live life with enthusiasm: I will only live once, so why not give it my all?

11. Enjoy life: I truly enjoy life.

12. Find a hobby you enjoy: No matter where I am, I have something I like to do.

13. Look for people to help: I get up every morning excited about the person I might help that day.

Answering life's final questions

Nate Meleen, a long-time friend who was also a neighbor when I was a boy, once told me, "My life's goal is that when I die, not one thing God has planned for me will be left unfinished." Now that is a great perspective!

When our goal is to accomplish God's will and hear, *"Well done, good and faithful servant!"* (Matthew 25:21), questions like "What

"If you are fortunate, someone with moral authority will ask you how you want to be remembered early enough in your life so that you will continue to ask it as long as you live."

Peter F. Drucker

do you wish you had done while you still could?" and "What do you want your epitaph to say?" will answer themselves.

When all is said and done, one final question remains: "How do I want to be remembered?"

That will show how you defined success.

Epilogue

Now you know what real success is. Will you open the success doors in front of you? Will you step through to find more than you can imagine, conceive, or dream?

It's up to you. It's your choice. You can, if you want to.

About the Author

Paul J. Meyer began his insurance career (1948-1957) immediately after military service and quickly became a top producer, leading two of the nation's largest life insurance companies. By age 27 he had acquired a personal net worth of $1,000,000 from personal production and agency development.

In 1960, Paul J. Meyer finally launched his dream business: Success Motivation International (SMI). Leadership Management, Inc. (LMI) followed soon after. These firms were established for the purpose of helping people develop their full potential.

For these companies, the product line over the years has expanded to include 26 full-length courses and programs in leadership development and management training. (**All of these programs contain printed and recorded materials and have combined sales of more than two billion dollars worldwide, more than any other author in this field, dead or alive.**) He is considered by many to be the founder of the personal development industry.

The Meyer family also owns and operates 40+ companies around the world, which include commercial construction, real estate development, legal insurance, auto racing, farming, computer software, printing, aviation, and more.

Paul J. Meyer has been instrumental in founding five charitable foundations to promote education and serve youth, including Passport to Success Foundation, Inc., which has helped provide post-secondary education to more than 1000 economically disadvantaged youth. Many of the other 30+ organizations and ministries across the nation and around the world that are supported by the Paul and Jane Meyer Family Foundation are mentioned in this book.

Although Paul J. Meyer claims he officially retired at age 70, he maintains his life-time goal of doing all the good he can, to as many as he can, for as long as he can. As a result, his vision for the future has only increased.

He says with passion, "The success I have achieved is only an inkling of what you are able to achieve!"

Acknowledgments

A lot of people helped to make this book a reality. They are:

Jane, my wife—your love and patience with me writing this, and every other goal and dream I've had, amazes me.

Karon Freeman and Linda Peterson, the best Executive Assistants in the world—your attention to detail, long hours, and constant encouragement are appreciated every day!

Hei Arita, business associate from Japan and long-time friend—thank you for all you do.

Dr. J. Clifton Williams—your 40+ years of friendship, counsel, and input have helped me in every area of life.

Nate Meleen, long-time friend and professor at Oral Roberts University—your great comments match your ability.

Brian Mast—your insights, suggestions, and edits have been invaluable in helping make this whole process a joy.

Harold and Grace Keown—your knowledge and experience were an added blessing.

Byron Weathersbee—thank you for all you do in helping people find real success.

You, the reader—your future is only limited by the degree of success that you choose!

Jesus Christ—You wrote our futures before the world ever was and You intend for us to succeed! The only way to say "Thank You" is to accept what You offer.

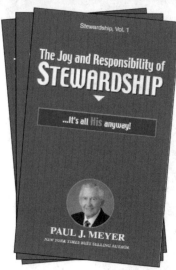
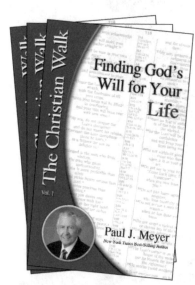

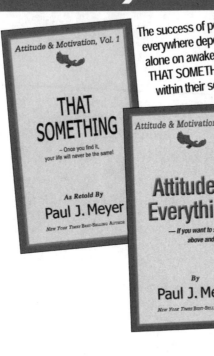

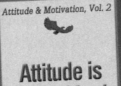